W9-BKU-540

The World in a Bowl of Tea

HarperCollins*Publishers*

The World in a Bowl of Tea

Bettina Vitell

Healthy,

Seasonal Foods

Inspired by

the Japanese

Way of Tea

FIRST EDITION

Designed and typeset by David Bullen

LIBRARY OF CONGRESS CATALOGING-IN-PUBLICATION DATA
Vitell, Bettina.
    The world in a bowl of tea : healthy, seasonal foods inspired by the Japanese way of tea / by Bettina Vitell.
       p.   cm.
    Includes bibliographical references and index.
    ISBN 0–06–018740–9
    1. Cookery, Japanese. 2. Cookery (Natural foods) 3. Japanese tea ceremony. I. Title.
    TX724.5.J3V57   1997
    641.5952—dc20   96–28146

---

97 98 99 00 01 ❖/RRD 10 9 8 7 6 5 4 3 2 1

For my mother, Elizabeth,
whose love of beauty and art has been an inspiration

In my own hands I hold a bowl of tea; I see all of nature represented in its green color. Closing my eyes I find green mountains and pure water within my own heart. Silently, sitting alone, drinking tea, I feel these become part of me. Sharing this bowl of tea with others, they, too, become one with it and nature.

Sōshitsu Sen XV

Contents

Acknowledgments

First and foremost my gratitude goes to Hounsai Oiemoto, the fifteenth-generation Grand Master of the Urasenke tradition, for sharing his vision of peace through a bowl of tea and for establishing Urasenke branches throughout the world.

My never-ending gratitude to Eido Shimano Roshi, Abbot of Dai Bosatsu Zendo and Shobo-ji in New York, for always encouraging me to seek the tenderness Dogen found after years of study in China, and for sharing with me the one true taste of Zen and Tea.

My deep gratitude to Christy Bartlett Sensei, director of the Urasenke Foundation of California and my teacher in the Way of Tea. This book could not have been written without her guidance and kindness.

Many thanks to Scott McDougall, the assistant director of the Urasenke Foundation of California, for his dedication to the Urasenke Foundation, for the many behind-the-scenes tasks that make Chanoyu so rewarding, and particularly for explaining to me over and over again the poetic names of objects, the way to tie boxes, where to find certain utensils in the often crowded kura, and for inventing the recipe for tomato sashimi.

Whenever I'm asked how I started to practice tea I seem only to remember where I began. My deep gratitude to the Urasenke Chanoyu Center in New York City and to Hisashi Yamada, Duane Feasel, and the late Michael Kane, who helped me on the way.

The San Francisco Shuchojo has evolved a wonderful group of students in the study of tea. I am very grateful to the senior students whose untiring and generous example in the kitchen, preparation room, and tea room continues to be an inspiration. Thank you to Kayoko Soga Fujimoto, Kyoko Sokyo Inouye, Setsuko Sosetsu Kuramoto, Sumi Honnami, Mutsuko Doyle, Suzuko Sorei Hasegawa, Eiko Soei Kajikami, Aiko Soai Umehara, and Maryann Soyo Goodman for your tremendous example in the Way of Tea. And many thanks to my dearest tea friends Randy Weingarten, Belinda Sweet, Mahoko Dahte,

Saori Nakashima, Dan Harvey, Dave Somers, Gary Barbaree, Michelle Ragland, Laurie Watanuki, Sonia Escaro, Akiko Sato, Aki Mori, Teri Reina, the late Jerry Fuller, and all the others who worked so hard in our impossibly tiny kitchen to make beautiful kaiseki food.

This book wouldn't be complete without mention of the wonderful gifts the mizuya and kitchen receive during tea gatherings. Sumi's sandwiches have nourished us over time. Mrs. Inouye's Jell-O has become famous, and we all hope "the three ladies" will arrive with sushi and other delectables. Freshly made fruit tarts still warm from the oven, cream puffs from a favorite bakery, and deviled eggs make our job a delight. Thank you to all the guests and friends who enjoy this tradition as much as we do.

A book is a collaborative effort. My heartfelt thanks to Susan Friedland, my editor, for having such a wide view of things as to accept my work. To her associate editor Jennifer Griffin for providing tremendous support, to Kathy Martin for editing the manuscript in such a clear-sighted way, and to David Bullen for the design.

Brian Wort of E-Media has helped me with computer and web design. Many thanks for all his support and enthusiasm for our many projects.

And most important, thank you to my dearest friend and partner, Ken McCarthy, whose support, teaching, and personal courage have inspired me to follow my dreams.

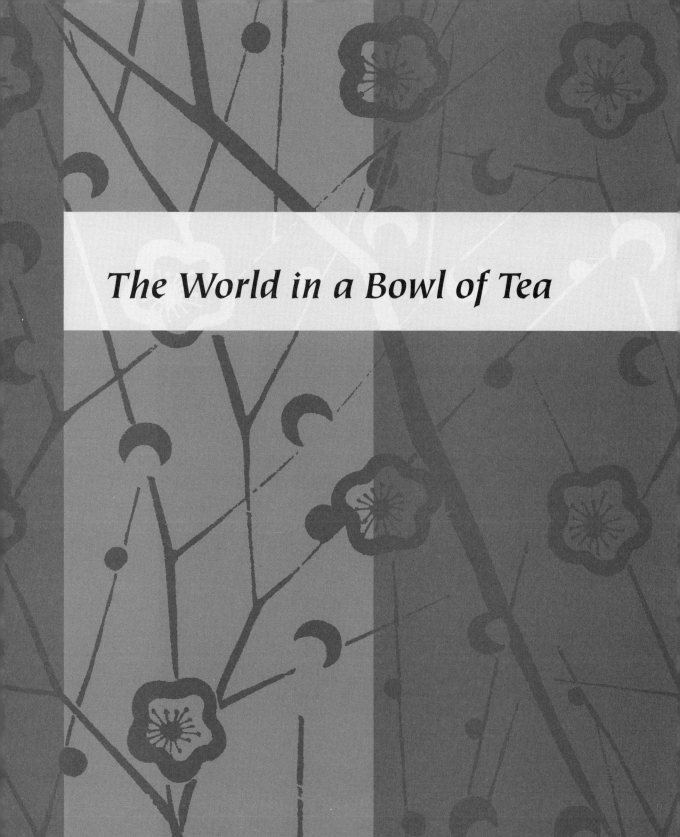

The World in a Bowl of Tea

Introduction

It is bright and clear this San Francisco morning as I arrive for my tea lesson. I climb the steps of an ordinary-looking building, walk through the door, and enter the world of tea. The fragrance of incense and the gentle rustling of my sensei's kimono greet me from behind the white paper doors of the tea room. I peer around the entrance and join her as she builds a fire in the sunken hearth. It is a perfect fire. She knows exactly where to lay the charcoal, and it burns with ruby red intensity.

I imagine my sensei at home in the deep woods, tending a campfire. I tell her this, but she says she can't imagine carrying heavy loads through the woods. We laugh at the thought of it, and it occurs to me that she doesn't need to go anywhere. She is already there.

This is the feeling of the tea room, the feeling deep at the core of Chanoyu, the Way of Tea. It is a place where, even in the midst of the city, you feel the peace and tranquillity of a mountain hut. A place where worldly cares disappear.

> Walking I reach where
> the waters well forth.
> Sitting, I watch the moment
> clouds arise.
> WANG WEI (699–759)

We sit quietly by the newly made fire and I feel our companionship. We don't need to go backpacking into the mountains. The great serenity and profound nature of mountain, desert, and ocean can be found here, in a single bowl of tea.

When Rikyu, Japan's legendary sixteenth-century tea master, was asked the secret of the Tea Ceremony, he replied, "Lighting the fire. Boiling the water. Whisking the tea." "Well, that seems easy to do," said the student. Rikyu responded, "If you can truly do this, then I will become your student."

The Way of Tea is a never-ending study. It is a practice of everyday life, and just as every day presents new situations and possibilities, so does a tea gathering. I've been studying Chanoyu on and off for more than ten years. This includes the connoisseurship of the fine and applied arts, flower arranging, garden design, architecture, literature, and Kaiseki cuisine. For the past four years, I've studied seriously in the kitchen, preparation room, and tea room of the Urasenke Foundation of California.

My studies have encompassed the writings of tea masters who have shaped and preserved the Way of Tea over the centuries. One of my favorite men of tea, Takeno Jo-o, wrote in his sixteenth-century *Letter on Wabi*, "Let there not be a single act divided from heart and mind." These words stay with me as I whisk a bowl of tea, clean the tea room, or prepare Kaiseki food.

Most of the menus and recipes here are ones I cooked while working at the Urasenke Foundation of California, and were created by Christy Bartlett and Scott McDougall. I've included others that seem to fit the Kaiseki philosophy of fresh, seasonal cooking. I've adapted the recipes to Western tastes, and have made them easy to prepare with familiar ingredients.

Although I've been a professional cook for many years, this book represents the beginning of my study of Kaiseki cuisine. Perhaps my experience will encourage you in your study of tea—a way to find beauty and tranquillity in everyday life; a way to live with simplicity and care for your surroundings, your friends, and ultimately the larger world.

It is said that "if the goodwill of the host is wholehearted, even a bowl of rice will seem delicious to the guest." I invite you to savor the recipes and writings that follow. It's my sincere wish that you enjoy the peace and serenity found in a bowl of tea.

In England, tea is served with milk and sugar. In India, it's mixed with spices and called chai. In America, it's brewed from bits of tea leaves in paper sachets with labels attached. In Japan, powdered green tea is whisked with hot water in ceramic bowls. Half the people in the world drink tea (one third drink coffee); after water, it's the world's most popular beverage.

Tea is grown on misty, cloud-covered mountain plantations in warm, humid climates with rich volcanic soil and plenty of rain. Aromatic Darjeeling from India, delicate Sencha from Japan, smoky oolong from Formosa (now Taiwan), and the thousands of other varieties all come from the same plant, the *Camellia sinensis*, a tropical evergreen with bright, shiny leaves. Like fine wine, tea from a particular region acquires a characteristic flavor depending upon climate, soil quality, and cultivation techniques. The processing method also influences flavor, and determines whether a tea is black, green, or oolong.

To produce black teas such as Darjeelings, Ceylons, and Assams, the leaves of the tea plant are spread in the open air for eight to twenty-four hours after harvesting to wither, dry, and oxidize. Then they're rolled in a big drum, which gently bruises the leaves to release enzymes. They ferment and turn copper and black, producing complex flavors and aromas.

Green teas such as the powdered Matcha for the Japanese Tea Ceremony are not allowed to oxidize. Immediately after harvest, the leaves are steamed to a bright emerald green, then quickly dried to preserve their fresh color and flavor.

Oolong teas such as peppery Formosa go through a combination of both processes, producing flavor characteristics of both black and green teas. The leaves are oxidized for a shorter time than those for black tea, partially fermented, and then dried.

Green tea has been drunk in Japan for eight hundred years. The many varieties and blends include nutty Genmaicha, which is often served in restaurants; smoky Hojicha; bittersweet Sencha; and rich Matcha.

For Chanoyu (the Tea Ceremony), finely ground Matcha is whisked to a rich green froth in hot water, producing a sort of Japanese cappuccino. For formal occasions, the best-quality Koicha (thick tea) is slowly whisked and kneaded to the consistency of creamy pesto sauce.

The best Matcha is grown south of Kyoto, in a mountainous area well protected from frost. Tea estates are as well known to tea connoisseurs as vineyards are to wine enthusiasts, and at every tea gathering the name of the tea and its blender are avidly discussed.

To understand why the green tea for Chanoyu is so highly prized, it helps to know something about the complex process by which it is produced. In April, when the first tea buds appear, the tea bushes are covered with reed matting and straw, supported by bamboo and wood frames. This protects the young plants from unexpected frost and overexposure to the sun. For about twenty days, the shaded buds slowly grow into leaves, developing flavor, aroma, and color.

After the tenth of May, the plump leaves are handpicked and immediately steamed to produce an emerald green color and sweet aroma. There are no set recipes, temperature gauges, or time charts to guide the chief processor; he relies on his sense of smell and years of experience to know when the leaves are done. Then they are sealed in large jars and placed in a cool storehouse for six months to mature in flavor.

In November the dried leaves are sorted and cut. After the stems, veins, and impurities are discarded, one tenth of the harvest remains. This tea is ground to a fine powder on a hand-carved stone mill.

The Matcha sipped in tea rooms is blended from many different leaves. Plants grown in red soil may produce a leaf with a rich, sweet taste but too yellow a color. A plant grown in sandy soil may have a perfect color but a weak taste. Tea growers sample as many as three thousand varieties of leaves before deciding on their subtle, sublime blends.

Tea had long been considered a medicine in China when Eisai, a twelfth-century Zen monk, brought green tea to Japan. Eisai praised it wherever he went, calling it an "elixir for the maintenance of life," particularly for sustaining the heart.

Modern scientific research supports that ancient belief. Green tea is rich in vitamins C and E and other nutrients that are lost to oxidation in black and oolong teas. One bowl of green tea a day contains enough fluoride to prevent tooth decay and strengthen bones. It has half as much caffeine as coffee, making it a stimulating yet soothing drink.

During their twenty days of covered cultivation, green tea leaves develop an abundant array of polyphenols (tannins), which give the tea its full-bodied flavor. These substances are known scientifically as antioxidants, and are thought to strengthen the immune system and aid in the prevention of cancer. United States and Chinese researchers recently concluded that drinking green tea can reduce the risk of stomach and esophageal cancer by half or more. Chinese medicines made from tea polyphenols are used to treat leukemia and chronic hepatitis.

Green tea also has been shown to reduce blood pressure, cholesterol, and arterial plaque. Researchers suspect that's one reason why a 1990 study found that Japan had half the rate of death from heart disease as the United States.

Twentieth-century scientists continue to explore the life-sustaining properties of tea that were extolled by a Zen monk eight hundred years ago.

How to Make a Bowl of Matcha

Warm a Japanese tea bowl or a cappuccino bowl with hot water. Empty and dry the bowl. Measure ½ teaspoon of powdered green tea into the bowl. Add ⅓ cup of water that is just below the boiling point. Use a bamboo whisk to whip the tea to a froth. Drink it right away, in three or four sips. (If it is sipped leisurely, the powder will settle to the bottom and the tea won't be as pleasurable.) Powdered green tea can be slightly bitter; serve a sweet with it to balance and complement its flavor.

Early Tea in Europe, China, and Japan

Like a great, mythical bear that has spent hundreds of years in hibernation, Europe awoke in the fifteenth century and looked upon a world of exploration, art, and riches far greater than any dream. Venetian bazaars traded goods from nearly every imaginable part of the world. The magical stories of great wealth and advanced cultures Marco Polo had brought back from the court of Kublai Khan 150 years earlier were a reality.

Tea and spices were worth their weight in gold. "Paradise Grains," a pepperlike spice from the deserts of Africa, disguised the taste of bad food. Cinnamon, cloves, and nutmeg from the East Indies seasoned foods with exotic flavors. Fragrant black tea, long prized as one of China's greatest treasures, became Europe's most popular nonalcoholic beverage. Tea transformed plain boiled water into a smoky, mysterious elixir. It boosted energy, and was advertised as a cure for hangovers and headaches.

Tea and spices were big business. English, Dutch, Spanish, Danish, Swedish, and French merchants formed rival East India companies to trade with China, Japan, and India. The companies grew rich and powerful. Governments authorized them to colonize foreign lands, negotiate peace treaties, and coin money. Merchant ships, built to carry large cargoes of tea, spices, silks, and gold, were manned with small fighting forces to ward off pirates and rival vessels.

By 1670, the Dutch East India Company was the richest corporation in the world. The money from its tea trade funded the culture of Rembrandt, Vermeer, and Frans Hals. At its peak, the company owned 150 trading vessels and 40 ships of war. There were twenty thousand sailors and fifty thousand civilians on its payroll; it paid an unprecedented 40 percent dividend to its stockholders.

The rival British East India Company built the greatest merchant ships of the time, the East Indiamen. Designed to withstand months-long voyages, they were outfitted with the best sails and supplied with enough arms to fight at least two full battles on the high seas. After stocking up with fresh fruits and supplies from the Canary Islands, off the African coast, they could make the six-month, 25,000-mile journey all the way to China without stopping.

British tea imports soared from 50 tons in 1700 to 15,000 tons in 1800. English promoters advertised tea as a health drink, and claimed it cured not only headaches but colds, dropsy, scurvy, and obstructions of the spleen and liver. A cup of tea was said to strengthen digestion and vanquish bad dreams.

Tea was the rage. Queen Anne of England drank it for breakfast instead of the usual ale. Men and women gathered in hundreds of coffeehouses around London to drink afternoon tea from tiny imported Ming porcelain cups. Londoners strolled through tea gardens and enjoyed tea and cakes in Chinese-style tea pavilions. High tea, with its silver service, porcelain cups, sandwiches, and cookies, eventually became a British national custom.

All the tea brewed in the Western world was grown only in China and exported from the tiny port town of Canton. Peasants cultivated it in small gardens deep in the Chinese interior. They sold the leaves to village tea purchasers, who sent them to district centers for sorting and blending. There the tea was packed into chests, wrapped with heavy matting, and loaded onto the backs of packhorses or coolies for the long journey over lakes, streams, and mountain passes to auction houses in Canton.

China felt culturally superior to Western "barbarians," and closed its doors to foreigners in 1520. Westerners were not allowed to venture beyond the waterfront streets of Canton. Despite the vast profits Europeans reaped from tea, they had no idea what a tea plant looked like, how tea was grown, or how it was blended and sorted. China held the secret to a billion-dollar business for three hundred years. European thirst for tea fueled the Opium War of 1839–1842, which forced China to open more port cities and contributed to its economic and political collapse.

The Chinese had cultivated and drunk tea for centuries by the time it reached Europe. Ancient Chinese texts attribute its discovery to an emperor in 2737 B.C. who was sipping boiled water in his garden when a leaf from a tea bush fell into his cup. Accounts of tea in 350 B.C. describe methods of boiling water and infusing leaves for a healthful drink. Fifth-century reports describe how tea leaves were pressed into cakes that were roasted and pounded into pieces. The pieces were put into a pot and covered with boiling water; ginger, onion, and orange were added to soften the bitter taste.

Tea became an established beverage in China during the great Tang dynasty (618–907), the golden age of literature and beauty. *The Classic of Tea*, written in 780 by Lu Yu, is a delightful account of tea practice, ritual, and aesthetic. He gives exacting instructions on the use of utensils and methods of brewing. Tea must be chosen for its delicacy, the water boiled to look "like pearls innumerable strung together." Teacups must be of a particular gray-green porcelain, the color perfect no matter how rare and priceless the cups. Above all, tea must be attended by beauty.

Tang China was the most sophisticated civilization in the world at that time, and it attracted Persians, Indians, Japanese, and others to its court. Travelers brought tribute of gold and silver, and new ideas from far-off lands. They traded for colored silks, translucent porcelains, fine paintings, and gleaming bronzes. Buddhist monks from India conversed with Taoist scholars. Students from Japan and other countries came to acquire knowledge. Zen Buddhism was vibrantly alive, taught by the most illustrious Chinese Zen masters of all time: Hyakujo, Obaku, Nansen, Joshu, and Rinzai.

Japanese Zen priests traveled back and forth to China, bringing home paintings, ceramics, lacquerware, and dyed silks. The journey was hazardous; typhoons sometimes capsized ships or swept passengers overboard. But the thirst for Chinese knowledge was insatiable. Chinese forms of religion, government, philosophy, and art were eagerly adopted by the Japanese. Tang palaces, court clothing, poetry, and calligraphy influenced ceremony, costume, literature, and writing in Japan. Even the capitals of Nara and Kyoto were modeled on famous Tang cities.

Tea was brought to Japan in 1191 by Eisai, the founder of Rinzai Zen Buddhism in Japan. Like other monks and scholars, he traveled to China to study Zen. There, in the great Sung temples, tea was part of the monastic ritual. Matcha, green powdered tea stirred in hot water with a bamboo whisk, kept the monks awake during long hours of meditation. When Eisai returned to Japan, he brought with him tea seeds that he planted on the grounds of the monastery Shofuku-ji. He gave seeds to his friend the Zen priest Myoe, who planted them at Togano-o on the outskirts of Kyoto. For two hundred years, the tea grown at Togano-o was considered the finest in the land.

Like most things imported from the continent, tea was something only the Japanese aristocracy could afford. They were eager for things modern and luxurious, and were swept up in a craze for Chinese tea objects. By the fourteenth century, the ruling lords of Japan were passionately collecting Chinese art. Tea bowls covered with jewel-like iridescent marks, bronze flower vases, and black-and-white Zen landscape paintings were the centerpieces for elaborate tea parties, displayed as symbols of wealth and connoisseurship.

Yoshimitsu (1358–1408), the third Ashikaga shogun and ruler of Japan, hosted lavish tea parties at his palace, the Golden Pavilion, outside Kyoto. Guests first viewed his Chinese art collection in a large gallery space on the ground floor. They marveled at his priceless treasures: exotic bronze incense burners, intricate ink landscape paintings, pristine ceramic tea bowls, and tiny tea caddies.

They adjourned to a banquet room, where they dined on sumptuous food and drank great amounts of sake. The guests then strolled through landscaped gardens and returned to the small top floor, designed like a Chinese scholar's study. Here they sat on tiger-skin rugs and drank as many as one hundred bowls of green tea, placing bets through the night on which was "real tea" from Togano-o. Winners received prizes chosen from the priceless objects displayed on the first floor.

These extravagant tea parties were gradually changed and simplified. Monks crossed class barriers and mingled with courtiers. Tea gatherings became occasions for discussing art, religion, and poetry. The elaborate banquet became a light meal with tiny cups of sake shared between host and guest. Lavish displays of art objects were distilled into a single Zen scroll and a simple flower arrangement. The Ashikagas' ostentatious parties were refined into elements of a tea gathering that can still be experienced today.

The Tea Aesthetic of Warriors and Artists

The fifteenth- and sixteenth-century world teemed with energy. In Europe, Columbus set sail for unknown territories, and Michelangelo sketched paintings for the Sistine Chapel. In Japan, half a world away, a century of civil war generated a renaissance of art and culture.

Chanoyu, the Tea Ceremony, developed in a country torn by war and bound by class barriers. The culture it created profoundly influenced the arts of Japan for centuries to come. Architecture, interior design, landscape gardening, cuisine, flower arranging, ceramics, and lacquerware were shaped by the artistic tastes and creativity of tea masters and warrior elite.

The ruling Ashikaga shoguns of the Muromachi period (1392–1568) built their wealth and power on lucrative but perilous commerce with China. Yoshimitsu also sought cultural power, and he used the lavish tea parties described in the previous chapter to showcase his incomparable collection of art treasures from the continent. Chinese art was rare and priceless, and gave its owner tremendous stature and influence.

By the time of the eighth Ashikaga shogun, Yoshimasa (1443–1490), Japan's wealthy aristocrats and warriors were feverishly collecting Chinese art for Chanoyu. Monochromatic Sung ink paintings by Mu Ch'i, Liang K'ai, and Yu Chien cost as much as ten thousand bolts of silk each. Such exorbitant prices encouraged forgeries, and wealthy households employed curators to authenticate new purchases and catalog collections of paintings and tea utensils. These connoisseurs became skilled in the art of Chanoyu, and thus, the first tea masters.

It was a time of ceaseless warfare. The ten-year Onin War (1467–1477) devastated the land and left the capital city of Kyoto burned to the ground. The emperor and his court were impoverished. Thousands of troops waged constant battle in outlying provinces. Despite the war, or more likely because of it, the arts flourished as never before during the late 1400s, known as the Higashiyama (Eastern Hills) period.

In 1474, the shogun Yoshimasa, as much an artist as a warrior, abdicated his rule and retired to his Silver Pavilion palace in the eastern hills of Kyoto. The art and culture he patronized embodied a new aesthetic, a retreat from the turmoil of the era. Yoshimasa's sense of beauty was greatly influenced by the tea master Murata Shuko (d. 1502), who introduced the idea that tea could go beyond lavish entertainment. Shuko articulated an aesthetic movement toward the simpler and more imperfect aspects of life: beauty in the plain; beauty of restraint that penetrates to the true essence of things. Yoshimasa was so impressed by Shuko that he wrote from his Silver Pavilion retreat, "If someone asks of me / tell him I am leading a simple life / in the mountains."

The tea aesthetic of the previous Kitayama era, the time of the Golden Pavilion, was characterized by elegance and sensual beauty. Through Shuko's influence, a restrained and refined aesthetic emerged. Sweeping Chinese landscapes gorgeously mounted in gold brocade were exchanged for more intimate views of nature; birds rising from a pond in an autumn sunset expressed the feeling of turning inward that characterized the time.

Shuko is said to have been a student of the great Zen master Ikkyu (1394–1481), who felt that tea drinking could be practiced as a way of Zen. Ikkyu encouraged Shuko to make tea a more spiritual art. Merchants, nobles, warriors, and artists were attracted to Zen. In war-torn Japan, they found refuge in the quiet elegance and peace of Chanoyu.

Shuko made innovative changes in the practice and perception of tea. He was the first host to personally make tea for his guests, using objects formerly kept in display cases. Tea bowls with glazes that resembled the feathers of a partridge or the fur markings of a hare, iron kettles with hailstone patterns, and small medicine jars filled with bright green powdered tea came alive with use.

Compared to the rich banquet rooms of the Silver Pavilion, Shuko's "grass hut" tea room was unimpressive. The nine-foot-square room, big enough for only four or five guests, was covered with straw tatami mats. The square lacquer posts and white papered walls created an impression of refined poverty, a setting in accord with the Zen attitude of naturalness, simplicity, and suggestion. The room was simply decorated, with a hanging scroll of calligraphy or a spray of flowers.

Shuko used Chinese objects the shoguns had rejected as too common; "Shuko celadons" are muddy and earthen rather than brilliant green. He is reported to have said, "The unclouded moon holds no interest," and he startled his guests by pairing rough Japanese wares with flawless Chinese ceramics, an aesthetic that heightened the beauty found beneath the surface of things. He valued human relationships and emotions more than sensuous objects; he was the first to display calligraphy of a Zen master with words that appealed to the spirit of a person.

His successor as the dominant arbiter of taste was Takeno Jo-o (1502–1555), a member of the upwardly mobile merchant and warrior class in the wealthy city of Sakai. Often compared with Venice of the same era, Sakai flourished as a center for armament production and trade with Ming China during the war-ravaged Sengoku period (1467–1568). Merchants amassed great fortunes, and sought the cultural legitimacy and power that had been the sole province of the aristocracy.

Urban retreats came into vogue in the merchant and warrior class. Their poetry and tea gatherings took place in thatched huts built in the back gardens of opulent city homes. With their simple materials and diffused natural light, these tea houses were like a mountain dwelling within the city, a peaceful refuge from the chaos of the times.

In this setting Sakai merchants and warlords avidly cultivated one another. Tea gatherings framed discussions of war and trade, but they also were occasions for the appreciation of art, architecture, interior design, food preparation, and gardening. Warlords and samurai considered accomplishment in tea or poetry as important as military training; hard-bitten warriors handled fragile tea bowls with the sensitivity of artists.

Connoisseurship of Chinese treasures still set the aesthetic standard; any tea man of worth owned at least one object from the dispersed Ashikaga collection. Like Shuko, Jo-o never rejected this tradition; he owned 650 Chinese objects, at least 60 of them from the Ashikaga collection. But through his unique perception of beauty, he reinvented the Chanoyu art form. He defined crude, "low tech" Japanese ceramics as *wabi,* a plain and unpolished beauty found in the irregular and unfinished qualities of an object. He paired a rough, dull brown Bizen water jar with a pristine Chinese tea bowl. He arranged freshly gathered flowers in a cracked and misshapen Shigaraki vase.

Jo-o also loved the fragile, courtly elegance of the bygone Hein era. He collected antique court objects and used them in the tea room in new and provocative ways: A small cosmetic case held tiny chips of sandalwood for incense; a red lacquer bucket became a jar for cold water. He mounted calligraphy by the thirteenth-century poet Fujiwara Teika in his tea room. A poem he loved to recite evokes a mood far different from Chinese landscapes and Zen calligraphy:

> *Gazing long to the shore*
> *There are no blossoms*
> *Or crimson leaves:*
> *Out at sea's edge, a rush hut*
> *In autumn dusk.*
> FUJIWARA TEIKA (1162–1241)

Elegance and artlessness, brilliance and plainness were compatible in Jo-o's eyes. His poignant love of the tranquil past combined with a Zen earthiness reflected the mood of his time.

The sixteenth century was the most brutal in Japanese history. In the morning a man might be your friend; by nightfall he could be your worst enemy. One of the most important figures of this turbulent time was Jo-o's student Sen Rikyu. Born in Sakai in 1522, he became the leading tea practitioner in the land.

Rikyu was tea master to two ambitious and powerful warlords, Oda Nobunaga (1534–1582) and Toyotomi Hideyoshi (1536–1598). Seeking to legitimize their power by demonstrating cultural knowledge and connoisseurship, both men practiced Chanoyu and avidly collected tea ware. Tea gatherings were not mere pastimes; they were often occasions when warlords and merchants met to form political and economic alliances. Tea caddies from the legendary Ashikaga collection were presented to the warlords as tokens of allegiance. The tiny glazed objects were worth fortunes, and gave their owners tremendous stature.

Nobunaga added to his collection by confiscating tea ware from vanquished foes. In what became known as the Meibutsu (Famous Objects) Hunt, he forced the merchants of Kyoto to surrender their famous pieces when he conquered the city in 1568. One enemy is said to have destroyed a treasured teakettle rather than relinquishing it to the warlord.

Hideyoshi's approach was more subtle. When he was a guest at a tea gathering, he would extravagantly admire the host's prized tea bowl or tea caddie. Often, the owner would later offer it to him as a gift.

Rikyu was able to balance the lavish tastes of his lords with his preferred *wabi* style. He paired precious Chinese tea utensils with found objects: a well bucket of plain wood, a charcoal container fashioned from a dried gourd, a flower basket designed from a fisherman's creel.

One of Rikyu's best-known innovations was the development of the Raku tea bowl. These works were created in collaboration with a local tile maker, Chojiro, and marked the first time a tea master designed a ceramic piece expressly for use in Chanoyu. Rough and natural, black and red, these bowls mirror the unpredictable beauty of stone.

He used everyday materials in new and different ways. He created flower vases from common bamboo. Once, Lord Hideyoshi tossed one of Rikyu's hand-carved vases out a window in displeasure. It cracked, but the tea master retrieved it and named it for the famous cracked temple bell at Onjoji. Rikyu used "Onjoji" often at his tea gatherings, and on one occasion a guest commented that it was leaking slightly. The tea master responded, "The dripping water is the life of the vase."

Rikyu took the concept of *wabi* further than his predecessors, creating a minimal, six-foot-square tea room with only two mats, one for the host and one for the guest. Coarse straw was left exposed on the roughly plastered walls, which were intersected by white papered windows much as in a modern painting by Mondrian. The room was so dark that one could barely make out the black tea bowl on the tatami mat. Smell, touch, and hearing became acute; the aroma of incense, the feel of the tea bowl, the sound of tea whisked in water were heightened by the dark intimacy of the room. Rikyu's environments were designed to minimize the distinction between outside and inside, worldly and spiritual, and to deepen the beauty found in simple objects of everyday life.

Rikyu's artistic vision, expressed through Chanoyu and its related arts, influenced every aspect of Japanese culture. The modern Japanese artist Teshigahara says, "What Rikyu did was total art. He initiated a new state of mind."

Like Shuko and Jo-o, he never rejected the aesthetic traditions of the past, but was able to bring them forward into a new age. His style was infused with a youthful vigor that embraced the beauty found hidden beneath the surface of things.

> *To one who awaits*
> *Only the cherry's blossoming*
> *I would show*
> *Spring in the mountain village,*
> *Its young herbs amid snow.*
> FUJIWARA IETAKA (1158–1237)

An Invitation to Tea

Chanoyu as it is practiced today had its beginnings in the tea rooms of Shuko, Jo-o, and Rikyu. The word *chanoyu* literally means "hot water for tea," and it is commonly translated in the West as "Tea Ceremony." But "ceremony" implies an unchanging form, a solemn rite, and Chanoyu is neither of these. It is a living art form that vividly reflects its changing milieu. At its heart is a simple, timeless human interaction: Friends gather to share a light meal and a bowl of tea.

Many of the elements of a traditional tea gathering can be incorporated in your own entertaining. To inspire your planning, read "Clouds and Brocade: Seasonal Notes" *(page 25)* and consider this description of an ideal tea gathering.

In summer, guests come early for tea, before the heat of the day. The garden is sprinkled with water; the stepping stones glisten in the early morning light, moist and cool like a path through a forest. There is a sense of bridging, crossing over, proceeding deep into the garden and leaving the dust of the world behind. The leaves rustle in the wind. A covered waiting area appears where the guests sip cool, freshly drawn water from translucent porcelain cups. Water drawn from the same source will be used later for the tea.

The tea house is made of the most ordinary materials: thatch, bark, reeds, bamboo, wood, paper, and clay. The entrance is low, a tiny door only two feet square. One by one, the guests approach a stone step, bend low, and scoot into a small room of shadow and light. They are greeted by the gentle sound of simmering water and the delicate aroma of sandalwood. A scroll hangs in the dimly lit alcove with words that speak of wind or water. Moistened reed blinds cover the windows, droplets of water glitter in the sun. The feeling is cool and refreshing. The guests sit quietly, absorbing the tranquil atmosphere.

In fall or winter, guests arrive in the late afternoon or evening. They make their way along a path scattered with red oak leaves. The tea room is warmed by oil lamps and candles, and the fragrance of aloe wood and clove fills the tiny space. The kettle simmers on a sunken hearth near the middle of the room. The guests gather close to watch as the host adds charcoal to the fire.

A light meal of hot soup, rice, grilled fish, and pickles is served on black lacquer trays and ceramic dishes. Sake is poured into shallow red cups. A cedar tray with delicacies from the mountain and the sea is passed. A stacked box filled with trufflelike sweets is left for the guests to eat. They adjourn to the waiting area, where they sit for a moment and enjoy the garden.

When the guests return, they find the tea room changed. In the alcove where the scroll had been there is now a simple flower arrangement in a bamboo vase—a maple branch and a white camellia. The kettle has been joined by objects used for making tea: a ceramic water jar and a small ceramic tea container encased in a silk bag. The mood of the gathering has deepened, and now all are silent.

The host enters the room with a single tea bowl. The sound of his feet brushing the tatami mats mingles with the gentle hissing of the kettle. His movements are rhythmic and smooth as he unwraps the tea container from the silk bag, wipes the bowl, scoops in powdered tea, and ladles water from the kettle. Movement to movement, the gestures seamlessly merge as he mixes the tea and water with a small bamboo whisk.

The tea bowl is placed in front of a guest. He picks it up. The rough black ceramic is like a warm stone in his hand, a landscape of emerald green tea inside. All is quiet: the taste of the tea, the company of others, the heart of the host. The words of the scroll still linger in the mind and lead to a deep feeling for things of the moment.

Kaiseki

The word *kaiseki* refers to the hot stones Zen monks wrap in the folds of their robes during long hours of meditation. They eat only two meals a day, in the morning and at noon, and the hot stones against their stomachs keep them from getting hungry. The Kaiseki meal served during the first part of a tea gathering is light, simple, and elegant, with just enough food to satisfy the guests before drinking tea. Kaiseki emphasizes the interaction of host and guest as more important than elaborate food and luxurious serving utensils. In the midst of scarcity, the host's sincerity is revealed.

Kaiseki has long been considered Japan's "haute cuisine." It is in keeping with modern interest in light, nutritious eating, and is similar in many ways to California cuisine. Both emphasize presentation and the use of high-quality seasonal ingredients. The food is never heavy or filling. Flavor, freshness, and appearance are paramount.

Seasoning is light: Avocado is dressed with lime; Chilean sea bass is charcoal-grilled with fennel seeds; spinach and crab are tossed with ginger vinaigrette. The clean, vibrant sauces and dressings never overshadow individual flavors. Oil is rarely used. Tastes are naturally balanced by combining flavors that are strong and delicate: salty and sweet, bland and tart.

Presentation is important, but you'll never find the elaborate garnishes and intricate arrangements you've seen in some sushi bars or trendy American restaurants. The spirit of Kaiseki is naturalness. A sprig of chervil or lemongrass, a few leaves of sorrel or strands of daikon sprouts add flavor, texture, color, aroma, and freshness. Slivers of lemon or lime, or citron zest evoke images of early spring, summer, or autumn.

Kaiseki cuisine is characterized by small, distinct courses served at carefully timed intervals. The host must sense the mood of the tea room, and allow just enough time between courses to create an atmosphere of anticipation and satisfaction. A typical menu consists of seven courses that are punctuated by servings of sake.

The first course is served on black lacquer trays. Each tray holds a small open dish containing a salad, perhaps finely sliced jicama and orange, and two matching covered lacquer bowls. The guests open the two lidded bowls at the same time. One contains a perfect line of white rice, and the other a creamy miso soup. The rice and miso complement each other; they are light and refreshing, and stimulate the appetite.

The host appears with an iron sake pot and tiny red lacquer cups. Each guest takes one, and the host pours what seems like a few thimblefuls of warm sake. More rice is served, and the miso bowls are refilled.

The second, or Nimono, course is swiftly brought into the room in lidded bowls. This dish, morsels of food in seasoned broth, is the heart of the Kaiseki meal. The guests bring the bowls close and remove the lids. The rising steam carries a delectable fragrance—lemongrass, perhaps. The clear broth might contain steamed fish, shiitake mushrooms, and parboiled spinach leaves, all in perfect harmony with the season.

The host enters again, with more sake, and after serving it to each guest, brings in a large dish of rough pottery that contains the third course. The Yakimono, a grilled food such as halibut or sea bass, is always served alone. Its delicate flavor is savored with a bit of grated citron or sansho leaves sprinkled on top.

The host returns to the kitchen, where he has a tidbit himself. Then he serves the fourth course, the Hashiarai, in small, lidded lacquer cups. Each one contains hot water flavored with a tiny sage blossom or a sliver of lemon to refresh the palate.

The fifth, or Hassun, course is the most poetic. A large part of its beauty is the tray. Until now, all the utensils have been ceramic or lacquer; the Hassun tray is almost always made of plain cedar, and its pale, straight grain is dampened just before serving. The tray contains two foods, one loosely classified as from the "mountain" and the other from the "sea," which are arranged in tiny piles to create contrasts of color, shape, texture, and seasoning. This could be asparagus tips paired with smoked salmon, or even melon slices with prosciutto. Although prosciutto is not literally a seafood, it creates the desired contrast of light and dark, sweet and salty. Each piece is intended as a single bite to accompany sake. The mood of the room is warm and convivial.

A sixth course, consisting of pickles and a last serving of rice, signals the end of the meal. The rice has continued to cook slowly, and by now it's crunchy and browned. The guests experience the passage of time with each serving of rice as its taste and texture changes. Pickles, chosen to reflect the season, cleanse the palate for the seventh and final course of sweets.

Like the food, the utensils and accessories for tea are chosen to match the occasion and subtly evoke the appropriate mood. At a spring gathering to celebrate the cherry blossoms, for example, the tea container is made of cherry wood, and the lacquer frame that surrounds the fire looks like a raft of blossoms floating on a river.

Utensils are also chosen for the way they harmonize and interact. In the West we prefer matched sets of dishes that vary only in size and shape. In tea, ceramic, wood, lacquer, bamboo, fabric, paper, and metal are all embraced. When highly polished lacquer is set against rough, sturdy pottery, the beauty of each object is enhanced. Disparity and contrast—this is where true harmony is found.

Often, a tea gathering includes at least one object that "challenges" the senses. A dull black tea bowl or a tarnished metal spoon will startle the eye. The same unexpected, astringent beauty can be found in the taste of the food, the color of the serving dish, the texture of the tea bowl, and the fragrance of the tea. But most important, it is found in the relationships created among these things.

For centuries, tea masters have understood that art can be found everywhere and appreciated in every aspect of daily life. We feel it vividly in the beauty of flowers placed in a vase, in the way a salad is arranged on a plate, and in the simple pleasure of making and drinking a bowl of tea.

Clouds and Brocade: Seasonal Notes

A famous porcelain bowl by Dohachi (1783–1855) is gloriously patterned with enameled maple leaves in bright reds, greens, and yellows on one side. As you turn the bowl, the pattern changes to a pale flurry of white and pink cherry blossoms. Men and women of tea have loved and copied this design for many years. It is called Clouds and Brocade, and it reminds us that even as winter approaches, there is spring to follow.

The circle of the seasons is one of the greatest teachings and pleasures of tea. It gently reminds us that the passage of time is impossible to grasp, fleeting as the cherry blossoms and maple leaves, yet there is always the feeling of the spring before and the spring to come.

Tea has a way of heightening the experience of nature, of its impermanence and ephemeral beauty. The tender beauty of a flower that lasts only a few hours or the gathering of friends in deep accord, never to be repeated, is often lost to us in the bustling pace of our lives. We grasp and try to hold on to what we think is beautiful, all the while missing what is right before us in the fleeting moment.

Kaiseki cooking is a wonderful place for you to begin appreciating the changing aspects of nature through the food you serve. In autumn, the markets are filled with squashes, pumpkins, and wild mushrooms. In summer, newly harvested corn, vine-ripened tomatoes, and brightly colored berries appear.

Miso soup, the rich, luxurious soup served as the first course of a Kaiseki meal, changes with the seasons. In deep winter, it is pale ivory, made with the finest sweet miso. As the weather warms, more and more red miso is added until finally, in the hottest month of the year, the soup is vividly red, rich, and salty.

Tea sweets are given poetic names that directly refer to the season. Snow on Brushwood or Brocade Jewel evoke emotional and seasonal experiences everyone can understand: the ephemeral beauty of melting snow, the moon shadowed by moving clouds, cherry blossoms lost in a flurry of petals, cool summer breezes.

Poetic references to Zen sayings, No plays, famous places, and well-known poems also play an important role in a tea gathering. The words of the scroll set the theme. The names of the tea bowls, flower vases, and other objects complement the words and imbue the pieces with aesthetic character. They create a story, a mood, that slowly, spontaneously reveals itself over the course of the gathering.

Use the seasonal references in the following pages in the same way you use images of the harvest to decorate your Thanksgiving table. Bring poetic images to your meal or tea gathering through your choice of foods, serving dishes, and decorations.

In summer, use a bowl with images of water and wind to create a cool feeling. Use cut glass or pale blue dishes with whirlpool patterns. Arrange flowers in baskets, and sprinkle water over black lacquer serving dishes to look like dew. In October, the most poignant month of the year, use objects that evoke memories, stories of cherished moments. Give the name Wind in the Pines to a tea scoop, or Quiet Retreat to a hand-shaped ceramic tea bowl. The names work together to create a theme of pilgrimage, a sense of turning inward.

Whatever mood you choose, bring together seasonal foods, serving dishes, utensils, paintings, flowers, and words to create a deep harmony of host and guest in this one ephemeral meeting, this one time together.

Autumn

Summer heat has broken. The moon is especially beautiful. Colored leaves on the mountains look like brocade. Days are getting cooler. Old letters are used as scrolls. Images of journeys. Putting things in storage. Time of outings and festivals. Last tea from the year's harvest. Baskets and rustic ceramics. A subdued feeling. A sense of not quite enough, yet savoring what remains.

Autumn foods: Sweet potatoes, chanterelle and lobster mushrooms, Yellow

Finn potatoes, sunburst squashes, spinach, eggplants, turnips, pumpkins, snow peas, lima beans. Chestnuts. Muscat grapes, cranberries, persimmons, Black Mission figs, raspberries, blackberries, yuzu. Oysters, scallops, crab, Pacific rockfish. Duck.

Flowers for the tea room: Pampas grass, mountain chrysanthemum, Japanese anemone, dianthus (pinks), bush clover, loosestrife, penstemon, feverfew, bell flowers, campanula, patrinia, toad lily, purple aster, knotweed. Baskets used the last time for the year.

> *harvest moon*
> *night brocade*
> *voice of autumn*
> *hunt for the moon*
> *first colored leaves*
> *cold dew*
> *sound of insects in autumn grasses*
> *river of memories*
> *wild geese crossing the autumn sky*
> *gifts from the mountains*
> *thin maple leaves*
> *wind parting the grass in the fields*
> *autumn colors on mountain ridges*
> *thatched hut*
> *path to the deep mountains*
> *white dew*

Winter

Snow viewing and "night-speaking" teas. Long evenings spent by the fire with close friends. Warm food and drink. A large fire in the hearth. The sound of water boiling in the kettle. Deep serving dishes with earthy glazes give a warm feeling.

Winter foods: Sweet potatoes, turnips, lotus root, and other root vegetables. Squashes, pumpkins, artichokes, eggplants, mustard greens, turnips, ginger, broccoli rabe. Soba noodles. Mandarin oranges, tangerines, pink grapefruit, kumquats, cranberries, Meyer lemons. Blue-skin fish from deep seas. Dungeness crabs, oysters, king salmon. Duck.

Flowers for the tea room: Peony and narcissus. All varieties of red, white, and pink camellia. In early November, white camellia called First Tempest with a branch of colorful Liquid Amber. Budding witch hazel, red-berried elder, dogwood branches. Closed-mouth vases with no view of cool water.

> *ageless mountain*
> *purity and tranquillity*
> *sleeping mountain*
> *ice flowers*
> *trees bent under heavy snow*
> *shadows are long*
> *sound of snow*
> *thick incense*
> *winter rain*
> *first dawn*
> *lingering snow*
> *putting on more layers of clothes*
> *long night*
> *icicles*
> *leafless trees*
> *bits of light ice drifting on the breeze*

Spring

Plants and grasses come alive. Flowers slowly open. Snow flurries. White against new green leaves. Swirling white plum blossoms scattering and falling. Evening cherry blossoms, black against white. Light spring mists and a brocade of mountain flowers.

Spring foods: Asparagus, Japanese eggplants, new potatoes, watercress, broccoli rabe, sugarsnap peas, spinach, artichokes, fava beans, sorrel, chervil, haricots verts. Mandarin oranges, strawberries. White miso. Salmon, bay scallops, clams.

Flowers for the tea room: Azalea, camellia, forsythia, pussy willow, witch hazel, viburnum, terrestrial orchid. Crab apple and mandarin orange blossoms.

> *flower snow flurry*
> *fragrant wind*
> *butterflies*
> *shells*
> *new green leaves*
> *bridge of dreams*
> *first goose*
> *young leaves reflected in green water*
> *raft of flowers*
> *plum viewing*
> *laughing mountains*
> *river of cherry blossoms*
> *spring mist*
> *flying plum tree*
> *banks of mist*
> *village of falling flowers*
> *shower of blossoms*
> *new grass in patches seen through snow*

Summer

Boats. Floating leaves. Rain showers. The plain cedar frame around the brazier is patterned with cutouts of reeds; a fresh breeze flows through the openings in the fragrant wood. Food for the dawn tea gathering is served in cut-glass dishes or dampened pottery. Dew settles on the black lacquer box for the sweets. Flowers in loosely woven baskets are still wet from the dawn.

Summer foods: Baby green beans, zucchini, squashes, squash blossoms, okra, Jerusalem artichokes, peppers, tomatoes, corn, avocados, jicama, fava beans, new potatoes, cucumbers, eggplants, okra, sage blossoms, lemon verbena, basil, arugula. Blueberries, raspberries, nectarines, figs, heirloom melons. Wild rice. Tart red miso. Salmon, tuna, halibut, rockfish, sea bass.

Flowers for the tea room: Columbine, evening primrose, balloon flower, dianthus (pinks), yarrow, bush clover, poppy, pine cricket grass, hydrangea, iris, larkspur, poppy, veronica, bachelor buttons, patrinia, Chinese meadow rue, rose of Sharon.

> *cool moss*
> *mountain streams*
> *pure water*
> *dense forest*
> *cottage overgrown with long grasses*
> *thunderstorm*
> *pine breezes*
> *evening shower*
> *water flowing through moss*
> *seashells*
> *singing frogs*
> *deep shade under trees*
> *whirlpool*
> *twilight*
> *fireflies and cicadas*
> *wind*
> *light*

Kaiseki Menus

Make a delicious bowl of tea; lay the charcoal so that it heats the water; arrange the flowers as they are in the field; in summer suggest coolness, in winter, warmth; do everything ahead of time; prepare for rain; and give those with whom you find yourself every consideration.

THE SEVEN RULES OF RIKYU

Hosting a tea gathering can be as simple as sharing sweets and whisked bowls of green tea with a friend or as elaborate as serving a seven-course meal for three to five guests. It's not hard to create these beautiful meals by incorporating elements of the tranquil mood, graceful style, and exquisite cuisine of a tea gathering into your everyday entertaining.

A formal tea gathering, or Chaji (*cha* translates as "tea"), lasts three to four hours. It involves the host, his or her assistant, three to five guests, and two or three kitchen helpers. A Chaji is sometimes described as a drama in two acts. In the first "act," the host builds a fire in the brazier or sunken hearth and serves the meal. Course follows course in quick succession, with sake served between them to provide phrasing. After the sweets are served, the guests adjourn to the garden. During this brief "intermission," the host swiftly changes the decoration of the room, replacing the scroll with flowers arranged as though growing wild in a field. The guests return. The second "act" is quiet and subdued as the host prepares and serves tea.

There are seven types of formal Chaji. For Asa Chaji, held in the hot summer months, guests enter the tea room at six o'clock in the morning. The coolness of the night still lingers. The food is light and refreshing; no raw fish or grilled foods are served. The gathering is timed to end just before the heat of the day.

In dark winter months, a Yobanashi Chaji, or "night-speaking tea," is held in the evening. The tea room, garden paths, steps, and waiting area are lit by candles and lanterns. The guests are given a hot drink before entering the tea room. The food is served in deep ceramic ware that holds the heat.

A Hango Chaji can be hosted in any season; it takes place before or after lunch. In this abbreviated form of Kaiseki, there are three or four courses: a soup, the cedar tray with foods from the mountain and sea, and sweets. Sometimes a light salad is also served.

In addition to the formal Chaji, there are less formal tea gatherings, called Tenshin Chakai (*tenshin* means "tray"). The guests enjoy a soup, tidbits of food served on a tray, sake, sweets, and tea. All the elements of a full Kaiseki meal are included, to produce a harmonious balance of textures, colors, and shapes.

Here are menus for a number of tea gatherings I helped to prepare at the Urasenke Foundation. (Many of the recipes appear, with slight variations, in the chapters to follow.) I offer them not as models to be strictly followed but as sources of ideas for planning your own tea gatherings or meals with a Kaiseki theme. I have also included the menu for a meal I enjoyed at a French restaurant to show how the Kaiseki style of small, simple, beautifully presented dishes can be adapted to many cuisines.

Chrysanthemum Tea Gathering

The Chrysanthemum Festival is celebrated on the ninth day of the ninth month. It is said that if you place cotton on the chrysanthemum overnight to soak up its dew and use it on your skin, you will enjoy eternal youth.

The theme of this tea gathering was the flower. Its image appeared in the rice, the pickles, the way the sunburst squash was sliced, the petals tossed with kiwi, and the sweets.

> *It must be because*
> *the autumn dew settles in*
> *various colors—*
> *the leaves of trees on distant*
> *mountains show a thousand hues.*
>
> ANONYMOUS, *Kokinshu Anthology, No. 259*

Tray

Rice with pale yellow sweet potato pressed into
chrysanthemum shape

Ginger flower pickle, plum pickle, chrysanthemum pickle

Chrysanthemum leaves with pine nut dressing

Sliced tofu roll

Smoked tuna

Kiwi tossed with lightly vinegared yellow chrysanthemum petals

Sake

Nimono (Morsels in Seasoned Broth)

Steamed halibut with cilantro

Sunburst squash sliced to resemble a chrysanthemum

Cinnamon cap mushrooms

Meyer lemon for fragrance

Sweets

Chrysanthemum flower sweets

Harvest Moon Tea Gathering

To celebrate the harvest moon in October, we held a tea gathering at Japonesque, a well-known San Francisco art gallery. Most of the serving dishes were from the gallery's collection of contemporary and traditional Japanese arts.

> *so taken with*
> *the faultless face and radiance*
> *of an alluring moon*
> *my mind goes farther . . . farther . . .*
> *to reach remote regions of the sky*
> SAIGYO (1118–1190)

Tray

Chestnut rice

Cucumber and plum pickles

Jicama, orange, and frisée with lime dressing and grated lime garnish

Sake

Oni Goroshi ("demon killer")

Nimono (Morsels in Seasoned Broth)

Shrimp dumplings

Lightly parboiled baby bok choy

Simmered shiitake mushrooms

Lemongrass for fragrance

Greens

Autumn greens and Fuyu persimmons dressed with seasoned vinegar

Foods from the Mountain and the Sea (Hassun)

Grilled figs with miso sauce

Grilled Chilean sea bass with Yuan sauce

Sweets

Pressed sweets in the shape of pinecones and bells of good fortune

Robiraki Tenshin

Robiraki, in November, is considered the tea person's New Year. It marks the beginning of the winter season, when the sunken hearth is opened in the tea room for the first time. The theme for this menu was influenced by autumn colors. It's the time of harvest, gourds, Thanksgiving turkey, and cranberry sauce. Orange chanterelles are in season and look beautiful in red soup bowls.

deep in the mountains
they have fallen with no one
to see their splendor —
these autumn leaves are a rich
brocade spread in the dark night.

KI NO TSURAYUKI (D. 945),
Kokinshu Anthology, No. 297

Tray

Rice with sweet potato in the shape of a gourd

Turkey marinated and baked in miso

Fresh cranberry relish

Takuan (daikon pickle) shaped like ginkgo leaf

Crab and spinach salad

Persimmons flavored with Meyer lemon

Truffle-shaped chestnut puree

Sake

Nimono (Morsels in Seasoned Broth)

Tofu dumpling

Carrots, Blue Lake green beans, and chanterelle mushrooms

Meyer lemon for fragrance

Sweets

Zenzai (sweet bean soup)

Hatsugama (New Year's Tea)

Hatsugama is the first tea gathering of the new year. The tea room is gorgeously decorated with symbols of good fortune. The red ceramic tea bowls are coated inside with a wash of silver and gold. Long branches of willow hang in the alcove, sweeping from ceiling to floor in one large, open knot. Knots are signs of good luck, and are found in many of the foods served during the meal. Two camellias, one each in the good-luck colors of red and white, are arranged in a bronze vase. To their right sits a tiny ceramic incense case shaped like an open fan, pointing outward to the infinite as a symbol of long life. Champagne is poured instead of sake for this Tenshin Chakai, and an extra course of food is served in stacked lacquer boxes.

In spring, cherry blossoms
in summer, the cuckoo
in autumn, the moon.
In winter, it is snow,
transparent and chill.
DOGEN (1200–1253)

Tray

Red rice pressed into the shape of plum blossoms

Tiny eggplant-mustard pickles

Smoked salmon rolled around daikon sprouts

Shrimp dumpling, triangular pickled cucumber, and squares of Wind in the Pine turkey skewered on a branch of willow with a knot on one end

Three black beans, burdock with sesame sauce, and kazunoko (fish roe) on a small round plate

Champagne

Miso Soup

Broiled mochi

Slices of fish paste (kamaboko)

Baby turnips with tops

Carrots cut in the shape of battle doors

Sprigs of chervil

Lemon peel cut in rounds for fragrance

Three Layered Boxes

First layer

Vinegared daikon cut like a chrysanthemum
and mustard greens with walnut dressing

Second layer

Potatoes cut in octagonal shapes and
carrots cut in the shape of plum blossoms

Third layer

Kumquats and sweetened black beans and
ornamental purple and white cabbage for garnish

Sweets

Hanabira Mochi, a special New Year's sweet consisting of pale pink
mochi wrapped in a half moon around sweetened bean paste and
candied burdock root

Pressed sugar in the shape of tiny boars for the Year of the Boar

Green and red ribbon candy tied in knots

Spring Shogo Chaji

Hosting a Shogo Chaji, a full seven-course Kaiseki meal, is a challenging but rewarding undertaking. It is said that while the guest's pleasure is three parts, the host's pleasure is seven.

> *The bridge of dreams*
> *Floating on the brief spring night*
> *Soon breaks off*
> *And from the mountaintop a cloud*
> *Takes leave into the open sky.*
> FUJIWARA TEIKA (1162–1241)

Tray

White Rice

Miso soup with Jerusalem artichokes

Mukozuke salad of crab with daikon sprouts dressed
with sweet vinegar

Sake

Nimono (Morsels in Seasoned Broth)

Diamond-shaped shrimp dumpling

Simmered shiitake

Mizuna greens with stems tied in knots

Seville orange cut in blossom shape

Grilled Tidbits (Yakimono)

Charcoal-grilled bamboo shoots with chopped sansho leaves

Light Broth to Clean the Palate (Hashiarai)

Seasoned hot water with salted cherry blossom

Foods from the Mountain and the Sea (Hassun)

Parboiled asparagus tips and dried shrimp

Pickles

Takuan cut in rectangles

Assorted pickles

Sweets

White, pink, and green trufflelike bean sweets called Robe of Flowers

Summer Hango Chaji

This simple, refreshing menu was one of my favorites to cook. We used some of the best foods of the season, and garnished the sweets with bits of clear kanten to look like dew scattered on top of hydrangea flowers.

Toy with flowers and their
fragrance scents your garments.
Scoop up the water,
the moon is in your hands.
KIDO CHIGU (1185–1269)

Mukozuke Salad

Galia melon (heirloom) sliced like sashimi and flavored with

lime juice and zest

Sake

Nimono (Morsels in Seasoned Broth)

Somen noodles

Zucchini

Grilled red trout

Minced sansho for fragrance

Foods from the Mountain and the Sea (Hassun)

Parboiled snow peas

Smoked trout

Sweets

Sweetened bean truffle in the shape of a pale pink hydrangea

Asa Chaji

This summer tea gathering begins just at dawn's light and ends by 9 A.M., so the guests can avoid the full heat of the day. The menu is light and refreshing, and the ancient Chinese words of the scroll add to the cool feeling of the gathering:

Moving clouds
running water

robes of dew
heart of the wind.

Tray

White rice mixed with wild rice

Red miso broth with triangular pieces of grilled polenta and
drops of mustard

Mukozuke salad of smoked Cajun catfish, arugula, and
red radish slices

Sake

Nimono (Morsels in Seasoned Broth)

Egg custard

Shiitake mushrooms

Slices of parboiled okra

Lemon verbena for fragrance

Light Broth to Clean the Palate (Hashiarai)

Sage blossoms in lightly salted broth

Foods from the Mountain and the Sea (Hassun)

Melon and prosciutto

Pickles

Takuan

Dilled green beans

Myoga

Sweets

Blueberry kanten Brocade Jewel

Autumn Tenshin Chakai

Two of us prepared this Kaiseki meal for the directors of the Urasenke Foundation before a board meeting.

> *The way of tea:*
> *trace it, and ever deeper it goes;*
> *like the fields of Musashi*
> *where the moon is lucent,*
> *its depths draw us on.*
> RIKKANSAI (1654–1726)

Tray

Rice with sweet potato in the shape of a gourd

Daikon pickles in the shape of chrysanthemums

Sweet citron pickle sliced in large triangles

Cooked kabocha pumpkin cut in wedges

Mukozuke Salad

Crab and spinach with ginger dressing

Nimono (Morsels in Seasoned Broth)

Shrimp and orange roughy dumplings

Carrot cut in plank shapes

Broccoli rabe

Meyer lemon for fragrance

Sweets

Sweets from Yamada Seika (a San Francisco sweets shop; see Suppliers, *page 195*)

Dinner at a French Restaurant

One of the best Kaiseki-like meals I have ever had was at Fleur de Lys, a four-star French restaurant in San Francisco. Each portion was only a few bites, but was impeccable in taste and appearance.

Appetizer

Puree of cauliflower

Tidbits of Food Served on a Black Patterned Plate

Parsnip flan

Paper-thin jicama folded around wild rice

Lentil salad wrapped with a thin slice of carrot

Small goat cheese pancake

Fresh Fruit Sorbet

Entree

Grilled sea bass

Assorted Desserts

How to Use This Book

Rikyu, the great tea master of the sixteenth century, believed that beauty has its most powerful effect when it arises from suggestion and restraint. He said, "A house should be just enough to protect you from rain, and food just enough to stop your hunger." In the same spirit, a Kaiseki meal should be simple in preparation and presentation, cooked with your heart, and planned for the pleasure of your guests.

Every dish in this book can be cooked and served in a beautiful way. The most important thing is the spirit you bring to it. A deep consideration for your guests is at the heart of a tea gathering, as it is at the heart of entertaining all over the world. The Kaiseki Menus *(page 31)* will help you plan your meals in this spirit; the foods and images suggested in Clouds and Brocade: Seasonal Notes *(page 25)* will help you create the desired mood.

The first step is to plan your menu. The basic Kaiseki meal is composed of a soup, three main dishes, and a sweet. Consider the season, the theme and hour of the gathering, and your guests' tastes. Above all, keep it simple. Even the great French chef Escoffier encouraged cooks to "Stay simple! Cook simply!"

The second step is to choose your ingredients. In Kaiseki cooking there is no need for elaborate techniques or sauces to enrich the already wonderful flavors of the season's best sweet peas, asparagus, or baby carrots. Look for locally grown produce. Farmers' and organic markets are wonderful places to find sweet, vine-ripened tomatoes, nutty-tasting wild mushrooms, or tart Meyer lemons. Choose the freshest and most beautiful vegetables, fruits, poultry, and fish you can find.

Next, choose your serving dishes. The famous modern Japanese potter Rosanjin began his career as a chef, and made bowls, cups, and plates for his restaurant. He said, "If clothes make the person, dishes make the food." And food arranged on his rough ware is beautiful indeed.

The dishes should give a strong sense of the season. For summer, use shallow wares with light, refreshing colors of celadon (pale green), white porcelain, and glass. Choose dishes that have designs of water or flowers. For a cooling feeling, serve smoked fish and radish slices on a bed of arugula, in pale blue antique luster glass. Or place steamed rice on a large green leaf in a basket. Delight your guests in autumn by arranging grilled mushrooms and greens in small dishes patterned with fall grasses. In colder months, choose softly glazed bowls that are warm to hold and deep enough to keep food hot. Serve sweets in a large dish with patterns of plum blossoms to anticipate the coming of spring.

The placement of food should be simple and natural. Think of creating a landscape of colors, shapes, and textures with your ingredients. Seasonal foods naturally produce wonderful color combinations. When arranged together on a black lacquer tray, sweet potato rounds scattered with black sesame seeds, two or three shiny green fava beans, slices of smoked trout and grilled eggplant, and a triangle of white rice mixed with chestnuts arouse the appetite by their beauty alone.

When arranging food on a tray or plate, avoid straight lines, equal triangles, and other symmetrical shapes. Place a square dish on a round tray or arrange square-shaped food in a round bowl. Leave space around the foods so that each element on the plate and the plate itself are distinct. Don't worry if the portions look small; the overall effect will satisfy the appetite—and you can always serve seconds.

Try using chopsticks for arranging food. They are designed to pick up bite-size pieces and will help you place the food in a natural way. Dishes with one ingredient or with two distinct ingredients, as in an Avocado and Grapefruit with Shiso, should be placed to the back of a small dish and piled in an overlapping fashion to form a cone shape. Foods that have been tossed with a dressing, such as Mustard Greens with Sesame Dressing, should be placed in a small mound on a plate or tray. Ingredients should rise slightly above the rim of a shallow dish, and two thirds of the way up the sides of a deep one.

Grilled foods that have been cut into pieces are often stacked casually in a large dish with lots of surrounding space. Rounds of sushi rolls are usually arranged like a pyramid, with three pieces on the bottom, two in the middle, and one on top.

Soups are generally served in lidded bowls, which are easy to find in

Japanese markets. The lids keep the soup piping hot. And it's a delight to uncover the bowls, discover the landscape inside, and smell the fragrant lemon or ginger.

One of the pleasures of tea is the freedom to use objects in a variety of shapes, materials, designs, and colors. At one tea gathering, fifteen sake cups were served on a large round tray. They were from different places, made in different kilns; some were old, some new, and one was of antique glass. The guests delighted in the variety as they picked their favorites.

Don't feel you need sets of black lacquer trays, Rosanjin plates, or Japanese lidded soup bowls for the menus in this book; there is freedom and eclecticism in the Way of Tea that allows the use of all appropriate wares, regardless of origin. Hosts often use utensils indigenous to their areas; in the Southwestern United States, for example, grilled squash is served in Santo Domingo pottery, and native flowers are arranged in Navajo baskets.

Experiment with dishes in your own collection, and search out beautiful objects that are made close to home. The vivid elegance of an antique blue-and-white dish used with a modern, flint gray lacquer bowl will leave a lasting impression of beauty with your guests. The delight is to mix the past and the present, the old and the new. Foods and utensils should flow together to create a harmony of color, shape, and texture appropriate to the season, the occasion, and the guests.

Basic Ingredients, Equipment, and Techniques

Ingredients

Soy sauce, tofu, fresh ginger, sea vegetables, and other Japanese ingredients have been familiar to vegetarians and natural foods cooks in this country for many years. Natural foods stores carry a large array of Japanese ingredients, and many large supermarkets devote whole sections to Asian foods. Even shiso leaf and aromatic yuzu citron are becoming more popular and widely available.

There are only a few Japanese ingredients that are essential for the recipes in this book. The most important is kombu, a wide, thick, dried seaweed. Without it your stocks will lack a unique and essential flavor. A good-quality soy sauce is also a must. Japanese cooks often use two or three different types. Light-colored usukuchi soy sauce is used for sauces or clear soups to avoid darkening the food. It is much saltier than regular soy sauce and should be used sparingly. Rice vinegar is a main seasoning ingredient for dressings and sauces. Use the finest quality you can find.

Refer to the Glossary *(page 189)* for details on favorite brands and types of foods, and Suppliers *(page 195)* for mail-order sources of kombu and green tea. When you shop for rice vinegar, soy sauce, or kombu in a Japanese market, most of the labels will be in Japanese, making the brands difficult to recognize. You won't go wrong if you buy the most expensive brand; the Japanese are honest about their pricing, and you can rely on the fact that the most expensive is the best.

Equipment

If your kitchen is already equipped with sharp knives and heavy-bottomed pots, you will need only a few Japanese utensils for the recipes in this book. They will add to your kitchen skills, and you will find many uses for them.

Suribachi: A suribachi is a glazed ceramic bowl with a rough, comblike interior that acts as a mortar. It comes with a wooden pestle, and is great for grinding seeds and nuts and for mixing sauce ingredients. Suribachis come in all sizes; I use a medium one, about 9 inches in diameter.

A food processor will substitute for a suribachi, but it often chops the food too fine. The suribachi gives you greater control over the texture of your sauces, and the smell of freshly roasted nuts and seeds ground in a suribachi is one of the great pleasures of Kaiseki cooking.

Fine-mesh sieves: Fine sieves with metal rims are used to strain soup stock, miso soups, and sauces. Cheesecloth can be substituted, but it's much harder to work with.

Steamer: For steamed fish, custards, and tofu rolls, you will need a large, layered steamer that will hold flat pans and plates. Japanese markets carry layered steamers made of metal; you can also use a Chinese bamboo steamer placed over a wok or large pot. (A basket steamer for vegetables will not substitute.) Always tie a cheesecloth on the underside of the steamer lid to prevent moisture from dripping onto the steamed foods.

Bamboo rolling mat: A bamboo rolling mat is indispensable for making sushi and other rolled foods. It is my favorite tool for preparing steamed greens: Roll the cooked greens in the mat, gently squeeze out the liquid, and unroll. Slice the greens into 1-inch lengths and toss with a sauce.

Ginger grater: Metal Japanese ginger graters have a well at the bottom that catches the juice. They finely grate fresh ginger and are much easier to use than regular graters.

Vegetable cutters and molds: Look for tiny metal cutouts in the shapes of triangles, circles, squares, and flower blossoms in Japanese kitchen supply stores. They come in sets and make wonderful seasonal garnishes from thin slices of carrots, radishes, or lemons.

Cooked rice is pressed into seasonal shapes in small individual rice molds that come in a variety of shapes. Cookie cutters may be substituted.

A square or rectangular pan with an insert that lifts out is useful for all sorts of dishes that are baked or steamed, then cut into square or triangular shapes. Many soup ingredients are cooked this way. See Suppliers (*page 195*) for sources.

Techniques

Preparing tofu: Tofu keeps fresh in the refrigerator for up to one week. Keep it covered with water, and change the water every other day. Always wash it in cold water before using.

Tofu must be pressed to eliminate excess liquid. To do so, place the block of tofu on a cutting board or cookie sheet with one end toward the sink. Raise the other end a few inches, and prop it up. Cover the tofu with another cutting board or a cookie sheet, and weight it with something heavy (I use cans of soup). Let the tofu drain for an hour.

Preparing ginger: Choose fresh ginger root that is firm and not wrinkled. Peel away the skin with a paring knife, and grate the ginger finely. To extract ginger juice, wrap the grated ginger in a fine tea cloth and squeeze the juice into a small cup. Discard the pulp.

Cooking rice and shaping it into molds: The most important tool for making perfect rice is a heavy-bottomed pot with a tight-fitting lid. Commercial rice cookers are an easy alternative.

For stove-top cooking, place short-grain Japanese rice and water in the pot, cover it, and bring it to a boil. When steam escapes from the lid, reduce the heat to low. Cook for 40 minutes. Rice essentially steams in the pot. Never open the lid to check on the rice or the steam will escape.

To mold the rice, line a cookie sheet with plastic wrap. Moisten the rice mold, and place it on the cookie sheet. Have a small bowl of water handy. Moisten a wooden paddle or spoon, and use it to fill the mold three fourths full with rice. Press down on the rice with the top of the mold to make a firm shape, but not too firm, or the rice will be hard to separate and eat. Lift the mold away from the rice.

Broiling mochi: Mochi are chewy rice cakes that come fresh or frozen. They are a wonderful ingredient in soups, and are best prepared in advance. Cut the cakes into quarters, and place them fairly far apart under a broiler. (The cooked pieces will stick to each other if they touch.) The mochi will puff up, expand, and brown very quickly, so keep your eye on them. Turn them to brown on the other side, and remove them to a plate to cool.

Roasting nuts and seeds: Roast nuts in a dry skillet over low heat. Keep tossing them so they roast on all sides without burning.

Recipes

Soups

Nimono (Morsels in Seasoned Broth)

In any cuisine, soups and sauces are the true test of a cook's ability. Nimono translates as "most important dish of seasoned broth," and the subtle broth with its various ingredients is the highlight of the Kaiseki meal. The ingredients—typically three or four seasonal foods—are steamed, grilled, or simmered separately to highlight their unique taste. The cooked ingredients are attractively arranged in the soup bowl, the broth is carefully poured in, and the soup is topped with a "fragrance"— an aromatic garnish such as grated fresh ginger, thinly sliced citrus zest, or sprigs of lemongrass or cilantro.

Nimono is served piping hot in tightly covered bowls. The guests bring the bowls close and lift the lids: They smell the fragrance; they see the glimmering landscape of color and shape created by the ingredients, and finally, they taste the sublime, deep flavor of the broth.

Some of the recipes may appear complicated, but the trick is to prepare most of the components of the soup in advance. Start the dashi broth first thing in the morning. Simmer the mushrooms, parboil the greens, broil the tofu, and so forth. Refrigerate the ingredients or keep them warm on the stove. Just before serving, reheat them if necessary (you don't want them to bring down the temperature of the broth), and assemble the soup. Prepare the fragrance at the very last moment to ensure its potency.

How to Prepare Citrus Fragrance

With a sharp paring knife, cut a lemon, lime, or yuzu (an especially fragrant Japanese citron) into eighths. Cut away all the fruit and white pulp until only the paper-thin skin is left. Cut it into strips about ⅜ inch wide and 1½ inches long. Cut down the middle of each strip, leaving ⅛ inch at one end. Tie the two ends together in a knot. Place it on top of the soup, and cover the bowl with a lid if you have one.

Dashi—Basic Stock

Dashi, a light fish stock, is a fundamental ingredient in Japanese cooking, and one of the most delicious stocks I've ever tasted. In Kaiseki cooking, dashi is used in Nimono and in miso soups, for sauces and dressings, and for flavoring simmered ingredients.

I encourage you to make this dashi for all the recipes in the book. You will be delighted with the results. It's easy, and takes only 45 minutes or so. You will need katsuo, or dried bonito flakes (see the Glossary, *page 189,* for details, and Suppliers, *page 195,* for sources), and a dried seaweed called kombu. Never wash or rinse kombu; simply wipe it lightly with a damp cloth before using.

Though it tastes best fresh, dashi is still superb when reheated. It can be refrigerated for a day or frozen for up to six months. I like to make a double batch and freeze the extra for convenience.

8½ to 9 cups broth

5 PIECES KOMBU, ABOUT 3 BY 5 INCHES EACH
10½ CUPS COLD WATER
5 CUPS (1.75 OUNCES) DENSELY PACKED KATSUO

In a large pot, heat the kombu and 10 cups of the water to just under a simmer. Cook for 25 minutes, making sure the liquid doesn't boil. Taste frequently as the flavors develop.

With tongs, remove the kombu from the pot and discard it. Add the remaining ½ cup cold water to the broth to bring its temperature down.

Add the katsuo, a handful at a time, allowing the flakes to settle into the water without stirring. Taste the broth after adding a few handfuls, then taste again when you've added all the katsuo. This will give you a sense of how the flavors develop.

Immediately remove the broth from the heat and strain it through a fine-mesh sieve.

Seasoned Dashi

An important element of all Nimono soups is lightly seasoned dashi. Whether made from katsuo stock or mushroom stock, the clear broth balances the strong and delicate flavors of the soup's main ingredients.

About 6½ cups broth

6 CUPS DASHI *(page 53)*
2 TABLESPOONS SAKE
PINCH OF SALT
3 TEASPOONS LIGHT SOY SAUCE

Heat the dashi to just under a simmer; never let it boil. Add the sake, salt, and soy sauce.

Mushroom Broth

If you don't have katsuo for the basic dashi, make this mushroom broth instead. Its clear, pure flavor reminds me of a delicate consommé.

About 9 cups broth

5 PIECES OF KOMBU, ABOUT 3 BY 5 INCHES EACH
2 LARGE DRIED SHIITAKE MUSHROOMS
10½ CUPS COLD WATER

In a large pot, bring the kombu, mushrooms, and water to just under a simmer and cook for 25 minutes, tasting frequently as the flavors develop. Make sure it doesn't boil. Remove and discard the kombu and mushrooms.

Seasoned Mushroom Broth

About 6½ cups broth

6 CUPS MUSHROOM BROTH *(page 54)*
5 TABLESPOONS SAKE
PINCH OF SALT
4½ TABLESPOONS SOY SAUCE

Heat the broth to just under a simmer, and add the sake, salt, and soy sauce.

Grilled Tofu, Chanterelle Mushrooms, and Broccoli Rabe in Seasoned Broth

This soup was served for a tea gathering in November. The cool autumn day was perfect for building a large fire in the sunken hearth and serving hot soup filled with wild mushrooms and other autumn delicacies. Select tender stalks of broccoli rabe about 4 inches long with tiny florets. Wild mushrooms vary in shape, size, and weight, and will cook down to about half their size. Select firm mushrooms that are large enough to cut into halves or fourths, for two large slices in each bowl of soup.

4 servings

8 TO 12 OUNCES FRESH CHANTERELLE MUSHROOMS

6 CUPS SEASONED DASHI *(page 54)*

8 STALKS BROCCOLI RABE

1 10-OUNCE BLOCK REGULAR TOFU, WASHED AND PRESSED *(page 49)*

4 KNOTTED STRIPS OF MEYER LEMON FRAGRANCE *(page 52)*

Clean the mushrooms with a damp paper towel, trim the stems, and cut the mushrooms lengthwise into halves or quarters.

Place the mushrooms and 1 cup of the broth in a small saucepan, and cook at just under a simmer for about 5 minutes, until tender. Strain the cooking liquid back into the remaining broth through a fine-mesh sieve. Set the mushrooms aside. (You will need 8 pieces for the soup; choose the most perfect ones, and save any extra for another use.)

Parboil the broccoli rabe in lightly salted water for about 5 minutes, until tender. Drain and set aside.

Preheat the broiler. Cut the pressed tofu into 6 2-inch squares. (You will have 2 extra squares; save them for another use.) Broil the tofu until golden brown, about 3 minutes per side. You may broil the tofu up to 1 hour in advance, place it in a shallow dish with a little broth, cover it with foil, and keep it warm in a low oven until serving.

To assemble:

Just before serving, heat the broth to just below a simmer; make sure it doesn't boil. Pour a tiny bit of it over the mushrooms and broccoli rabe to heat them.

For each serving, place 1 piece of warm tofu toward the back of a soup bowl. Place 2 mushroom pieces against the tofu, and 2 stems of broccoli rabe over the top.

Pour hot broth against the side of the bowl so as not to disturb the arrangement of the ingredients. Add enough broth to come to the shoulders of the tofu. Place the lemon fragrance on top, cover the soup bowls with lids if you have them, and serve immediately.

Herbed Fish in Seasoned Broth with Sunburst Squashes, Wild Mushrooms, and Lemon

Small yellow sunburst squashes with tiny bits of green around the stem are perfect for a late-summer tea gathering with a chrysanthemum theme. When sliced across the top, the squashes, also called pattypan, resemble the flower. Cilantro brushed on the fish looks like a carpet of green in the soup. You may substitute any wild mushroom in season for the cinnamon caps.

4 servings

> ½ POUND CINNAMON CAP MUSHROOMS
>
> 4 SUNBURST SQUASHES (ABOUT ½ POUND)
>
> 12 OUNCES FILLET OF ORANGE ROUGHY, HALIBUT, RED SNAPPER, OR OTHER MILD WHITE FISH
>
> 2 EGG WHITES, WHISKED UNTIL FROTHY
>
> ⅓ CUP CHOPPED FRESH CILANTRO
>
> 1 CUP UNSEASONED DASHI *(page 53)*
>
> 6 CUPS SEASONED DASHI *(page 54)*
>
> 4 KNOTTED STRIPS OF LEMON FRAGRANCE *(page 52)*

Wash the mushrooms, and reserve any blemished ones for another use. Divide the remaining mushrooms into 4 clumps, enough for 2 or 3 bites per serving.

Cut the squashes across the tops into ¼-inch slices.

Wash the fish, salt it lightly, and refrigerate it for about 30 minutes. Rinse it well, and cut it into 4 pieces that will fit in the bottom of the soup bowls. Place the pieces in small, individual heat-proof saucers. Brush the fish all over with egg white, and cover the tops with a thick layer of cilantro.

Place the dishes in a heated steamer (*see page 48*), and cook the fish for 10 minutes. (Be sure to wrap a cloth under the steamer lid to prevent moisture from dripping on the fish.)

While the fish is steaming, simmer the squashes in lightly salted water just until tender, about 5 minutes.

Place the clumps of mushrooms in the unseasoned dashi and gently cook for 5 minutes.

In a large pot, heat the seasoned dashi to just under a simmer; make sure it doesn't boil.

To assemble:

For each serving, place 1 piece of fish toward the back of a soup bowl. Place 2 slices of squash against the fish, with the stem end of the second slice facing the front. Place a clump of mushrooms on top.

Ladle enough hot broth against the side of the bowl to almost cover the ingredients. Place the lemon fragrance on top, cover the soup bowls with lids if you have them, and serve immediately.

Clear Shiitake Consommé with Pumpkin Ravioli

This autumn combination of amber broth flavored with sake and sweet orange pumpkin cooked in homemade pasta is delectable. Ravioli is perfectly suited to traditional Japanese Nimono, which often has dumplings as its main ingredient. Serve this soup in large white brasserie bowls if you have them. You can prepare the broth, pasta dough, and squash in advance to save time when you assemble the dish for serving.

4 servings

1 KABOCHA PUMPKIN OR ACORN SQUASH (ABOUT 2 POUNDS)

½ TEASPOON SALT

1 TABLESPOON SAKE

1 TEASPOON SUGAR

For the pasta:

1 CUP UNBLEACHED ALL-PURPOSE FLOUR

1 EGG, SLIGHTLY BEATEN

1 TEASPOON OLIVE OIL

SALT

To finish the dish:

6 CUPS SEASONED MUSHROOM BROTH *(page 55)*

4 SPRIGS TREFOIL OR CHERVIL FOR GARNISH

Preheat the oven to 450° F. Line a baking sheet with parchment paper.

Cut the pumpkin in half, and place it facedown on the prepared baking sheet. Bake it until soft, about 15 minutes.

Scoop out and discard the seeds and fibrous pulp. Scoop out the flesh, and mix it with the salt, sake, and sugar. Set it aside or cover and refrigerate it until needed.

To make the pasta dough, put the flour in a large bowl, and make a well in the center. Pour the egg into the well, and stir with a fork, incorporating it into the flour a little at a time. If the dough is too dry, add water, a teaspoon at a time, until it holds together. (Don't add too much; wet, sticky dough is hard to work with.)

Turn the dough out onto a floured surface, and knead it for about 10 minutes, until smooth and elastic. Wrap it in plastic wrap, and let it rest for 45 minutes. (It can be refrigerated for up to 8 hours.)

On a lightly floured work surface, divide the dough into thirds, and flatten each third into a rectangle. Roll each piece of dough through a pasta machine, beginning with the widest setting. Continue to roll it through the machine, reducing the setting until the dough is a thin, transparent sheet about 5½ inches wide.

Dust a baking sheet with flour and set it aside.

Lay out one dough sheet on a floured work surface. Starting about 1 inch from the bottom and side edges, place dollops of pumpkin filling about 2 inches apart in a single row along the length of the dough. Use a pastry brush dipped in water to moisten the bottom edge and the spaces between the filling. Fold the top portion of the dough over the filling so that the top and bottom edges meet. Press firmly between the dollops of filling to seal each ravioli. Use a ravioli cutter to cut the ravioli into 2½-inch squares. Repeat with the remaining dough sheets and filling.

Set the finished ravioli on the baking sheet, cover with wax paper, and refrigerate until needed.

Add the oil and a little salt to a large pot of water, and bring it to a boil. Cook the ravioli for 5 minutes, until tender. (There will be extras in case your guests ask for seconds.)

Meanwhile, heat the broth in another large pot to just below a simmer; don't let it boil.

To assemble:

For each serving, place 2 ravioli in a soup bowl. Ladle the broth on top, garnish with a sprig of trefoil, and serve immediately.

Seasoned Broth with Tofu Dumplings, Spinach, and Ginger

These dumplings also make a wonderful appetizer served with Soy-Ginger Dipping Sauce (see Note).

6 servings

2 LARGE, DRIED SHIITAKE MUSHROOMS

1 BLOCK FIRM (16 OUNCES) TOFU, WASHED AND PRESSED *(page 49)*

2 EGG WHITES

1 TABLESPOON SUGAR

1 TABLESPOON ALL-PURPOSE FLOUR

⅛ TEASPOON SALT

½ CUP FINELY CHOPPED CARROTS

1 CUP CANOLA OIL FOR FRYING

6 CUPS SEASONED DASHI *(page 54)*

12 BABY SPINACH LEAVES WITH 1-INCH STEMS

2 TABLESPOONS PEELED AND GRATED FRESH GINGER

Soak the mushrooms in warm water until soft, about 30 minutes. Squeeze them dry, discard the stems, and chop the mushroom caps finely.

Mash the tofu in a food processor or suribachi until smooth. Add the egg whites, sugar, flour, and salt, and combine well. Stir in the mushrooms and carrots. Form the mixture into balls a little bigger than walnuts. You will have about 18.

Heat the oil in a deep cast iron pot or frying pan over high heat until the surface begins to ripple; don't let it boil. Fry 3 to 4 dumplings at a time, turning them so they brown all over. It will take about 3 minutes per batch. Drain on paper towels, and reheat the oil to just below a simmer before adding the next batch. This will keep the dumplings from absorbing too much oil.

Heat the dashi in a large pot to just below a simmer; don't let it boil.

Blanch the spinach leaves in boiling water for a few seconds. Set them aside. (If the spinach is cooked ahead, reheat it with a few drops of hot broth.)

To assemble:

For each serving, place 2 dumplings toward the back of a soup bowl. Arrange 2 spinach leaves in front, resting against the dumplings. (If your soup bowls are large, use 3 dumplings, and arrange the spinach leaves across the top.) Ladle broth against the side of the bowl, being careful not to disturb the ingredients, until it almost covers the dumplings. Place a small mound of ginger on top. Cover the soup bowls with lids if you have them, and serve immediately.

Note:

To make Soy-Ginger Dipping Sauce, stir together 1 heaping tablespoon grated fresh ginger and ¼ cup soy sauce. Serve in individual saucers.

Somen Noodles with Zucchini and Grilled Trout in Seasoned Broth

Somen noodles with grilled fish make a light, refreshing summer meal. Fresh sansho, a wonderful aromatic leaf, highlights this dish with its fragrance.

6 servings

3 TROUT FILLETS WITH SKIN (5 OUNCES EACH)

SALT

2 MEDIUM ZUCCHINI

8 OUNCES SOMEN NOODLES

6 CUPS SEASONED DASHI (*page 54*)

MINCED FRESH SANSHO LEAVES OR GRATED LEMON ZEST

Prepare a charcoal grill. Thirty minutes before grilling, wash and salt the trout. Cut each fillet in two, and fold each piece in half so the skin is on the outside. Insert 2 metal skewers into each piece; if the skewers are long enough, each pair can hold 2 or 3 pieces of fish.

Slice the zucchini into ½-inch rounds, and bevel the edges slightly. About 10 minutes before serving, parboil the zucchini in lightly salted water until cooked but still firm, 3 to 5 minutes. Remove it from the heat and let it stay warm in the cooking liquid.

Bring about 5 cups of water to boil for the noodles. As the water is heating, place the fish on the grill very close to the fire and cook for 1 or 2 minutes per side, until the skin is crisp.

Add the noodles to the boiling water, and cook for 1 minute. Remove the pot from the heat, and add ½ cup cold water to stop the cooking.

To assemble:

For each serving, use chopsticks or tongs to grasp a portion of noodles (enough for 4 or 5 bites) and lay them in the back of a soup bowl like a ribbon, a top layer over a bottom layer. Place 1 piece of grilled fish on top of the noodles. Place 3 zucchini rounds at the front of the bowl, leaning them against the noodles.

Ladle in just enough broth to almost cover the ingredients. Top with a mound of minced sansho leaves or grated lemon zest. Cover the soup bowls with lids if you have them, and serve immediately.

Flavored Custard and Green Beans in Seasoned Broth

This delicate custard, seasoned only with broth, is one of my favorite dishes. The bright green beans and slivers of lemon make a beautiful landscape of color and shape arranged in red lacquer soup bowls.

6 servings

6 EGGS, LIGHTLY BEATEN

2 CUPS UNSEASONED DASHI *(page 53)*, CHILLED

1 TEASPOON SOY SAUCE

PINCH OF SALT

9 GREEN BEANS, TRIMMED AND SLICED IN HALF LENGTHWISE

6 CUPS SEASONED DASHI *(page 54)*

6 SIMMERED SHIITAKE MUSHROOMS *(page 130)*, HEATED

6 KNOTTED STRIPS OF LEMON FRAGRANCE *(page 52)*

Stir the eggs into the cold dashi. Season with the soy sauce and salt. Pass the mixture through a fine-mesh sieve, and pour it into a 6-by-5-inch rectangular mold with a removable insert. (Or use a rectangular baking dish of about the same size lined with foil extending a few inches over the two short ends.)

Heat 1 inch of water in a steamer over medium-low heat. Wrap the lid with a cloth to prevent water from dripping into the custard. Steam the custard for about 20 minutes, until firm, keeping the heat low enough to prevent it from bubbling.

Parboil the green beans in lightly salted water for 1 or 2 minutes until bright green. Drain, and set aside in a shallow dish.

Heat the dashi to just below a simmer; don't let it boil.

Remove the custard from the steamer. Slide a knife around the edge, and lift out the insert or aluminum foil. Cut the custard into 6 squares, big enough for two or three bites each.

Rewarm the beans if necessary with a few drops of hot broth.

To assemble:

For each serving, place 1 square of custard toward the back of a soup bowl. Place a mushroom against the front of the custard. (If it's big, cut it in two.) Place 3 green bean halves across the top.

Ladle the broth against the side of the bowl so as not to disturb the arrangement; add enough broth to almost cover the ingredients. Garnish with the lemon fragrance. Cover the soup bowls with lids if you have them, and serve immediately.

Egg Custard, Shiitake, Okra, and Lemon Verbena in Seasoned Broth

This version of the traditional Tamaga Dofu, as it's known in Japan, is perfect for a light, elegant summer meal. The fragrance of lemon verbena was especially refreshing at a dawn tea gathering where this was the main dish.

6 servings

6 EGGS, LIGHTLY BEATEN

2 CUPS UNSEASONED DASHI *(page 53)*, CHILLED

1 TEASPOON SOY SAUCE

PINCH OF SALT

8 TO 10 MEDIUM OKRA

6 CUPS SEASONED DASHI *(page 54)*

6 SIMMERED SHIITAKE MUSHROOMS *(page 130)*, WARMED

6 FRESH LEMON VERBENA LEAVES

Stir the eggs into the cold dashi. Season with the soy sauce and salt. Pass the mixture through a fine-mesh sieve, and pour it into a heat-proof 6-cup mixing bowl.

Heat 1 inch of water in a steamer over medium-low heat. Wrap the lid with a cloth to prevent water from dripping into the custard. Steam the custard for about 20 minutes, until firm, keeping the heat low enough to prevent it from bubbling.

While the custard cooks, trim the tips from the okra, but don't cut off the stems. Parboil the okra in lightly salted water for about 5 minutes, and drain. When cool enough to handle, cut the okra in half on the diagonal, and set them aside in a shallow dish.

Heat the dashi to just below a simmer; don't let it boil.

Remove the custard from the steamer.

Pour a little hot broth over the okra to rewarm it.

To assemble:

For each serving, scoop out a large serving-spoonful of custard against the side of the mixing bowl, and place it upside down in the center of a soup bowl.

Place a mushroom against the front of the custard. Place 2 slices of okra, cut sides toward the front, against the mushroom.

Ladle in the broth against the side of the bowl so as not to disturb the arrangement; add enough to come up to the shoulders of the custard.

Slap each lemon verbena leaf in your hand to release the fragrance, and place one on top of each custard. Cover the soup bowls with lids if you have them, and serve immediately.

Shinjo with Spinach and Lemongrass

A Nimono with shinjo—seasoned broth with dumplings—is one of the dishes perfected in Kaiseki cuisine, and no Kaiseki cookbook would be complete without it. These dumplings are made of shrimp and orange roughy. They turn a pale pink, and look beautiful arranged in broth with spinach and a sprig of fresh lemongrass for fragrance.

6 servings

6 OUNCES MEDIUM SHRIMP

6 OUNCES ORANGE ROUGHY OR HALIBUT

1 EGG WHITE

1 TEASPOON ARROWROOT POWDER

¼ TO ½ CUP UNSEASONED DASHI *(page 53)*, CHILLED

8 CUPS SEASONED DASHI *(page 54)*

6 SPRIGS OF LEMONGRASS

12 SPINACH LEAVES

Peel and devein the shrimp. Wash the fish and pat it dry. Process the shrimp and fish in a food processor for about 5 minutes, until it forms a smooth, somewhat glutinous paste.

Add the egg white and arrowroot powder, and process until well blended. Thin with just enough chilled dashi to make a firm paste that will hold its shape.

Dilute 3 cups of the seasoned dashi with 1 cup of water. Heat it in a large saucepan to just below a simmer; don't let it boil.

Dip two large spoons in cold water. Use one to scoop out a heaping tablespoonful of dumpling paste. Use the other spoon to smooth the top of the paste into a rounded shape, and slide it into the hot broth. Repeat with the rest of the paste, dipping the spoons in cold water each time. You will have about 12 dumplings.

Regulate the heat to keep the dashi at just below a simmer. Poach the dumplings, uncovered, for about 10 minutes, until they have almost doubled in size and roll over easily.

While the dumplings are cooking, peel and discard the outer skin from the lemongrass, and trim each leaf into a 2-inch piece. Leaving a fraction of an inch at the end, slice each piece into 4 fanlike strands. Wrap them in plastic wrap.

Heat the remaining 5 cups seasoned dashi to just below a simmer; make sure it never boils.

Parboil the spinach in lightly salted water for 1 minute.

To assemble:

For each serving, remove 2 dumplings from the poaching liquid with a slotted spoon, and place them toward the back of a large soup bowl. Place 2 spinach leaves against the front of the dumplings. Pour hot broth against the side of the bowl so as not to disturb the arrangement of the ingredients. Add enough broth to come up to the shoulders of the dumplings. Lay a sprig of lemongrass on top, cover the bowls with lids if you have them, and serve immediately.

Variation:

Pour the uncooked dumpling paste into a 5½-by-6-inch pan with a removable insert. Place the pan in a steamer over medium-high heat and cook for about 15 minutes, until firm. Run a knife around the edges of the pan, and lift out the insert. Cut the dumplings into 6 squares, and cut each square in half on the diagonal to form triangle shapes. Use 2 triangles in each large soup bowl.

Miso Soups

A small portion of miso soup is served at the beginning of a Kaiseki meal. The thick, velvety soup contains two or three bites of seasonal food that rise slightly above the liquid and are often topped with a drop or two of mustard to brighten the flavor. Three azuki beans or small greens are typically added for contrasting taste and texture.

The passage of time, so appreciated in tea, is evident in the changing ingredients and flavors of the soup. In cold weather, the soup is traditionally made with sweet white miso. As the weather warms, more and more salty red miso is added until finally, at midsummer, only red miso is used. As summer fades and the weather cools, the red miso is diluted with white.

The secret to a good miso soup is the quality of broth and miso. The soup's thick, creamy texture is produced by straining it through a fine-mesh sieve several times. If you have broth on hand, it doesn't take much time to make the soup, and it's a unique delicacy that is sure to endear you to your guests.

Miso Soup with Baby Turnips, Carrots, Chervil, and Lemon

This creamy white soup, filled with colorful ingredients, is a favorite New Year's Day dish, served with other delicacies and champagne (see Kaiseki Menus, *page 31*).

6 servings

 2 CUPS PALE YELLOW OR WHITE MISO

 7 CUPS UNSEASONED DASHI *(page 53)*

 6 WHOLE BABY TURNIPS WITH TOPS

 3 LARGE CARROTS

 1 LEMON

 12 BITE-SIZE PIECES OF MOCHI, LIGHTLY BROILED *(page 49)* *(optional)*

 12 FRESH CHERVIL SPRIGS

Use a suribachi or food processor to blend the miso until smooth. Add the dashi a little at a time, processing until well blended. (Work in batches if your processor isn't big enough to hold all the liquid.) Strain the soup through a fine-mesh sieve three or four times, until velvety smooth. Transfer it to a soup pot.

Trim the tops of the turnips to 1 inch. Peel the shoulders of the turnips so they are snow white. Parboil them in salted water for about 10 minutes, until almost tender.

Peel the carrots, and cut them into paper-thin rectangular slices about 3 inches long and ½ inch wide. (You will need 12 slices; choose the most perfect ones, and save the rest for another use.) Parboil the carrots in salted water for about 3 minutes, until almost tender.

Cut the lemon in half lengthwise, and cut each half into thirds. Remove and discard the fruit and pulp. Place each piece of peel against a cutting board, and use a sharp paring knife to cut away the white pulp, leaving only the paper-thin skin. If you have a small, round cutout, use it to cut a round from each wedge of peel.

Heat the miso soup to just below a simmer; don't let it boil.

To assemble:

For each serving, place 2 pieces of warm mochi toward the back of a soup bowl. Place a turnip and 2 carrot slices against the mochi. Add enough soup to almost cover the vegetables. Garnish with 2 sprigs of chervil, and top with a round or wedge of lemon peel. Cover the bowls with lids if you have them, and serve immediately.

Variation with broccoli:

Substitute 12 steamed broccoli florets for the turnips.

Miso Soup with Sweet Potatoes

The touch of red miso gives this early-spring soup a little bite.

6 servings

 3 LARGE SWEET POTATOES (ABOUT 1½ POUNDS)
 2 CUPS SWEET WHITE MISO
 1 TABLESPOON RED MISO
 7¼ CUPS UNSEASONED DASHI *(page 53)*
 1 TABLESPOON DRY MUSTARD

Cut the sweet potatoes into 1½-inch-thick slices. Parboil them until cooked through but still firm, 10 to 15 minutes, and drain. When cool enough to handle, peel the slices and trim their edges to form diamond shapes.

Use a suribachi or food processor to blend the white and red miso together until smooth. Add 7 cups of the broth, a little at a time, mixing well. (Work in batches if your processor isn't large enough to hold all the liquid.) Strain the soup through a fine-mesh sieve three or four times, until velvety smooth. Place it in a soup pot, and heat it to just below a simmer. Make sure it doesn't boil.

Meanwhile, mix the dry mustard with enough soup to make a thick paste. Allow it to sit for 10 minutes. Just before serving, thin the mustard paste with a little more soup so that it will drop off the edge of a spoon or chopstick.

Heat the remaining ¼ cup dashi to just below a simmer, and pour it over the potato slices to warm them.

To assemble:

For each serving, place 2 sweet potato slices in a soup bowl. Pour in enough soup to come to the shoulders of the sweet potato. Drop a bit of mustard on top. Cover the bowls with lids if you have them, and serve.

Miso Soup with Pumpkin

Make this soup in the autumn with newly harvested pumpkins or squashes. Kabocha pumpkins and acorn squash look wonderful with their autumnal colors. The acorn squash has a ruffled fan shape that is especially pleasing. As the weather cools, white miso is added to the red for a refreshing complement to the sweet pumpkins.

6 servings

½ POUND KABOCHA PUMPKIN OR ACORN SQUASH

9 CUPS UNSEASONED DASHI *(page 53)*

1 TABLESPOON MIRIN

1 TABLESPOON SOY SAUCE

½ CUP RED MISO

1 ½ CUPS WHITE MISO

1 TABLESPOON DRY MUSTARD

Cut the pumpkin or squash in half. Scoop out and discard the seeds and fibrous pulp. Cut the flesh and rind into quarters, and then into wedges about 2 inches long and 1 inch wide. If using kabocha pumpkin, peel away all but a few strips and bits of the green peel to create a camouflage-like pattern. The slight peel will keep the pumpkin from disintegrating as it simmers.

Place the pumpkin in a medium saucepan with 2 cups of the broth and the mirin and soy sauce. Simmer for 15 to 20 minutes, until tender but still firm enough to hold its shape.

Use a suribachi or food processor to blend the red and white miso together until smooth. Add the broth a little at a time, mixing well. (Work in batches if your processor isn't big enough to hold all the liquid.) Strain the mixture through a fine-mesh sieve three or four times until velvety smooth. Place it in a soup pot and heat to just below a simmer. Be very careful not to boil it.

Meanwhile, mix the dry mustard with enough of the soup to make a thick paste. Allow it to sit for 10 minutes. Just before serving, add a little more soup to thin the mustard so that it will drop off the edge of a spoon or chopstick.

To assemble:

For each serving, place two pieces of hot pumpkin, skin side up, in a soup bowl. Pour in enough soup to come up to the shoulders of the vegetable. Drop a bit of mustard on top, cover the bowls with lids if you have them, and serve.

Miso Soup with Grilled Eggplants

Markets offer all sorts of varieties of eggplants in late October and November. Dark purple Japanese eggplants are small enough to serve whole in a bowl of soup. Tart red miso is mixed with the sweet white miso to give a robust flavor to the soup.

6 servings

> 6 SMALL JAPANESE EGGPLANTS
> ½ CUP RED MISO
> 1½ CUPS WHITE MISO
> 7 CUPS UNSEASONED DASHI (*page 53*)
> 1 TABLESPOON DRY MUSTARD

Prepare a charcoal fire in a grill or preheat the broiler. Grill or broil the whole eggplants about 4 inches from the heat for 8 to 10 minutes, turning them several times, until the skin is blackened and the flesh is soft. Plunge them immediately into cold water. Peel off the skin and cut off the ends.

Use a suribachi or food processor to blend the red and white miso together until smooth. Add the broth a little at a time, mixing well. (Work in batches if your processor isn't big enough to hold all the ingredients.) Strain the mixture through a fine-mesh sieve three or four times, until velvety smooth. Place it in a soup pot and heat it to just below a simmer. Be very careful not to boil it.

Meanwhile, mix the dry mustard with enough of the soup to make a thick paste. Allow it to sit for 10 minutes. Just before serving, add a little more soup to thin the mustard so that it will drop off the edge of a spoon or chopstick.

To assemble:

For each serving, place a grilled eggplant in a soup bowl. Pour in enough soup to come to the shoulders of the eggplant. Drop a bit of mustard on top. Cover the bowls with lids if you have them, and serve.

Recipes

Tomato "Sashimi"

Galia Melon with Lime

Tuna and Curly Endive with Lemon

Smoked Cajun Catfish, Arugula, and Radishes

Crab with Grilled Mushrooms and Sorrel

Shrimp and Jicama with Ginger Vinaigrette

Crab and Spinach Salad with Persimmon

Baby Artichokes with Pomegranate Vinaigrette

Tofu with Sesame Ginger Sauce

Shrimp and Cucumber with Sesame Vinaigrette

Smoked Salmon Rolls with Daikon Sprouts

Avocado and Grapefruit with Shiso

Jicama, Orange, and Frisée

Sun-Dried Tomatoes with Cucumbers and White Dressing

Apricot and Turnip Salad

Salads

At a Chaji, the full-course Kaiseki meal, a black lacquer tray holding two matching covered lacquer bowls and an open dish called a mukozuke centered in the back is brought to each guest. In Japanese, *muko* means "far side" (as in the far side of the tray) and *zuke* or *tsukeru* means "small portion." I have loosely titled this chapter Salads, based on this dish.

The essence of the mukozuke is freshness. Traditionally, the main ingredient is sashimi, raw sliced fish, lightly dressed with vinegar or citrus and garnished with a seasonal green. In this chapter you won't find any sashimi, which is best left to professional chefs, but you will find refreshing dishes that reflect the clean, pure tastes of the mukozuke. Transparent slices of grapefruit dressed with fresh lime juice, crab and spinach tossed with ginger, and thin wedges of tomato arranged with watercress are sashimi-like in their freshness and appearance.

One of the great pleasures of the mukozuke is the serving dish itself. Its color, shape, and design provide a dramatic contrast to the black lacquer tray and lidded bowls. In summer, use cut glass or blue-and-white porcelain to give a feeling of coolness. In winter, use stoneware to convey a sense of warmth. The famous Japanese potter Kenzan made small muko-zuke dishes in the shape of maple leaves. Others are in the shape of camellias or open fans, or have designs of flowers and grasses painted on them. Choose your dish to match the season.

This first-course salad awakens the palate. The dressing is simple, sometimes just fresh lemon or lime juice, which never overshadows the flavors of the main ingredients. Carefully arrange the salad in the dish. It should not look too hearty; it's an invitation for the courses that follow. The dressing is usually poured on the side of the dish so the guests can mix the ingredients and wasabi (Japanese horseradish) to suit their taste. The mukozuke is served with warm sake, which complements the fresh, piquant tastes of the salad.

Tomato "Sashimi"

Flavorful tomatoes are sliced with the same care and attention as the raw fish for traditional sashimi. Choose fruity, vine-ripened tomatoes at their peak.

4 servings

4 MEDIUM RIPE TOMATOES
4 TABLESPOONS FRESH LIME JUICE
2 TEASPOONS SOY SAUCE
PINCH OF SALT
1 TABLESPOON WASABI POWDER
12 SPRIGS WATERCRESS

Bring a large saucepan of water to the boil. Plunge the tomatoes in for just a moment. Rinse them under cold running water, and peel them. Cut the tomatoes into quarters, and remove the seeds. Slice each quarter into thin wedges. Cover and chill for 30 minutes.

Mix the lime juice, soy sauce, and salt in a small bowl.

In another small bowl, combine the wasabi with just enough water to form a doughlike paste. Mold the paste into 4 small pyramid shapes.

Divide the tomato wedges among 4 small plates. Top each with 3 sprigs of watercress. Place a wasabi pyramid on one of the sprigs. Drizzle the lime sauce on the side of the dish so that it forms a pool. Serve immediately.

Galia Melon with Lime

Serve this refreshing salad on small blue and white plates for an early-summer meal; it goes especially well with a soup of grilled fish and somen noodles. Slice the melon paper thin to resemble sashimi.

4 servings

1 MEDIUM GALIA MELON OR CANTALOUPE
2 LIMES

Cut the melon into quarters. Peel and seed it. Cut the quarters into paper-thin strips. Trim them into quarter-moon shapes. Cover and chill for 30 minutes.

Just before serving, grate the zest and squeeze the juice from the limes. Divide the melon slices among 4 small plates, twisting them into spiral shapes. Sprinkle the melon with the lime juice and garnish it with the lime zest. Serve immediately.

Tuna and Curly Endive with Lemon

Tuna, often served raw as sashimi, is lightly grilled or broiled for this first-course salad.

4 servings

  1 LARGE RED BELL PEPPER
  1 LARGE YELLOW BELL PEPPER
  1 ½ TEASPOONS SUGAR
  ¼ CUP FRESH LEMON JUICE
  1 TEASPOON SOY SAUCE
  12 OUNCES TUNA FILLET
  CANOLA OIL
  SALT
  8 CURLY ENDIVE LEAVES

Roast the peppers under a broiler or over a flame on the stove top, turning often until the skin is blistered and blackened on all sides. Put them in a paper bag, close it tight, and let the peppers steam for 15 minutes. Peel, stem, and seed the peppers, and slice them into thin strips.

Stir the sugar, lemon juice, and soy sauce together in a small bowl until the sugar is dissolved.

Prepare a fire in the grill or preheat the broiler.

Rinse the tuna, and pat it dry. Brush it lightly with the oil, and sprinkle it with salt.

Grill or broil the fish 3 or 4 inches from the heat for about 1 minute on each side. The tuna should be slightly rare in the middle and charred on the outside. When it's cool enough to handle, cut it into thin slices.

Divide the tuna and peppers among four bowls or plates, carefully overlapping the slices to form a mounded shape. In a deep bowl, the food should come to just below the edge; in a shallow bowl or plate, it should rise just above the rim. Leave empty space on all sides of the food.

Garnish each salad with 2 leaves of curly endive. Pour the lemon dressing to the side of the mounded food to form a small pool. Serve immediately.

Smoked Cajun Catfish, Arugula, and Radishes

Smoked catfish gives a Southern accent to an early-morning summer tea. To create cool scenery, arrange this salad in antique pale blue luster-glass dishes. Carry out the theme with later courses of okra and wild rice.

4 servings

> 4 OUNCES SMOKED CAJUN CATFISH
>
> 4 TO 6 TINY RED RADISHES
>
> 1 LARGE LEMON
>
> 12 TO 16 UNBLEMISHED ARUGULA LEAVES, CHILLED

Cut the catfish into strips about ½ inch wide and 1½ inches long. Cover and refrigerate for 30 minutes.

Slice the radishes into paper-thin rounds, and cover them with cold water.

At serving time, drain the radish slices, and juice the lemon. For each serving, place 3 or 4 arugula leaves on a small plate. Top the arugula with one quarter of the fish strips, arranging them in an overlapping fashion to form a mound. Garnish the fish with 3 or 4 radish slices, drizzle it with lemon juice, and serve immediately.

Crab with Grilled Mushrooms and Sorrel

Fresh shiitake or chanterelle mushrooms are wonderful in late fall in this tart, refreshing salad. Serve it on plates patterned with autumn grasses.

6 servings

½ POUND COOKED KING CRAB LEGS IN THE SHELL

6 FRESH CHANTERELLE OR SHIITAKE MUSHROOMS

SALT

4 TABLESPOONS FRESH LEMON JUICE

4 TABLESPOONS SOY SAUCE

A SPLASH OF MIRIN

1 TEASPOON SUGAR

18 SORREL LEAVES

Carefully remove the crabmeat from the shell, leaving the leg meat intact as much as possible. Tear the rest of the crabmeat into bite-size portions.

Prepare a fire in the grill.

Wipe the mushrooms with a damp paper towel. Remove and discard the stems. Salt the mushroom caps lightly. Grill them, stem side first, for 2 to 2½ minutes per side. Or cook them in a little oil in a skillet over medium-high heat for about 2 minutes per side. Be careful not to overcook, or they will dry out and lose their flavor. Cut the mushrooms in half.

Stir together the lemon juice, soy sauce, mirin, and sugar in a small saucepan, and cook over medium heat until the sugar dissolves. Cool to room temperature.

Place 3 sorrel leaves in each of 6 small dishes. Divide the crabmeat among the dishes, piling the small pieces and overlapping the leg meat to form a mounded shape. Place 2 mushroom halves at the front of each mound. Drizzle the salad with the cooled dressing, and serve immediately.

Shrimp and Jicama with Ginger Vinaigrette

The clear, pure taste of jicama is perfect for Kaiseki cuisine. Here it's tossed with shrimp and seasoned with soy sauce and ginger juice.

4 servings

For the vinaigrette:
- ⅓ cup rice vinegar
- 1½ tablespoons sugar
- ½ teaspoon salt
- ½ teaspoon soy sauce
- 1 teaspoon ginger juice *(page 49)*

For the salad:
- 3 cups unseasoned Dashi *(page 53)* or water
- 16 medium or large shrimp, peeled and deveined
- ½ pound jicama, peeled and cut into julienne (about 1½ cups)
- 2 cups watercress or small spinach leaves

To make the vinaigrette, whisk together the rice vinegar, sugar, salt, soy sauce, and ginger juice until the sugar is dissolved.

Heat the dashi to just below a simmer, and poach the shrimp for about 5 minutes, until they turn bright pink. Drain, and refrigerate for 30 minutes.

Toss the chilled shrimp with the jicama.

For each serving, arrange a quarter of the watercress leaves in a small dish or bowl. Heap a quarter of the jicama and shrimp on top, paying careful attention to the balance of the surrounding space. Arrange the food to evenly distribute color and shape. Drizzle with the vinaigrette, and serve immediately.

Crab and Spinach Salad with Persimmon

In November, when the air is crisp and cool, the large sunken hearth in the tea room is used for the first time. Crab is at its freshest, and this salad is always a big hit at the tea gathering held to celebrate the first fire of the new season. See *page 48* for information about the bamboo rolling mat.

4 servings

For the dressing:

⅓ CUP RICE VINEGAR

1½ TABLESPOONS SUGAR

½ TEASPOON SALT

½ TEASPOON USUKUCHI (LIGHT) SOY SAUCE

For the salad:

1 POUND SPINACH

1 FUYU PERSIMMON

JUICE OF 1 MEYER LEMON

1 POUND COOKED CRABMEAT

To make the dressing, whisk together the rice vinegar, sugar, salt, and soy sauce until the sugar dissolves. Set the dressing aside.

Steam the spinach until it just begins to wilt. Drain and set it aside to cool.

Spread half the spinach in a strip across a bamboo rolling mat, about 2 inches from the bottom. Fold the bottom of the mat over the spinach, and roll away from you, pressing firmly. When you come to the end of the roll, twist it over the sink to squeeze out all liquid. Press the roll back into shape, and unroll it. Cut the rolled spinach into 1-inch pieces, and transfer them to a mixing bowl. Repeat with the remaining spinach.

Peel the persimmon, cut it into eighths, and sprinkle it with the lemon juice.

Pick through the crabmeat and discard any bits of shell. Toss it with the spinach and dressing.

Mound the crab mixture onto individual plates or bowls. Garnish each portion with 2 persimmon slices, and serve immediately.

Baby Artichokes with Pomegranate Vinaigrette

Delicate baby artichokes and ruby red pomegranates are irresistible in November and early December. Serve this jewel-like salad on small blue-and-white porcelain plates. The flavoring is very light; the best-quality rice vinegar will make all the difference.

4 servings

> JUICE OF 1 LEMON
>
> 6 BABY ARTICHOKES, ABOUT 2 INCHES IN DIAMETER
>
> ⅓ CUP RICE VINEGAR
>
> 2 TABLESPOONS SUGAR
>
> PINCH OF SALT
>
> 24 TO 32 POMEGRANATE SEEDS

Fill a 4-quart pot with water, and add the lemon juice.

Trim the tips of the artichoke leaves. Cut off the stems and remove the tough outer leaves. Cut the artichokes in half, and remove the tiny chokes. Immediately place them in the acidulated water. Bring it to a boil, reduce the heat, and simmer for about 30 minutes, until the artichokes are tender.

Meanwhile, mix the vinegar, sugar, and salt in a small saucepan and cook for a minute or two over low heat until the sugar dissolves. Cover and refrigerate.

For each serving, arrange 3 artichoke halves on a small plate. Garnish each portion with 6 to 8 pomegranate seeds. Drizzle with the sweetened vinegar, and serve immediately.

Tofu with Sesame Ginger Sauce

I ate this "temple food" at a Zen retreat. The cook prepared this simple dish often, and I never got tired of it. Use the freshest, most savory tofu possible; the ginger sauce brings out its delicate flavor.

4 servings

1 ½ TABLESPOONS SESAME SEEDS

2 TEASPOONS FINELY GRATED FRESH GINGER

¼ CUP SOY SAUCE

2 BLOCKS (10 OUNCES EACH) FIRM TOFU, PRESSED AND DRAINED
(*page 49*)

24 TO 32 SPINACH, WATERCRESS, OR FRISÉE LEAVES

Roast the sesame seeds in a dry skillet over low heat for 2 or 3 minutes, until they begin to pop and give off a delicious aroma.

Grind the seeds lightly in a suribachi or food processor. Add the ginger and soy sauce, and mix well.

Cut the tofu into rectangular ¼-inch-thick slices.

For each serving, arrange 6 to 8 spinach leaves on a small plate. Arrange one quarter of the tofu slices on top. Serve the ginger-sesame sauce in a separate bowl, to be spooned over the tofu.

Shrimp and Cucumber with Sesame Vinaigrette

The tart vinaigrette and cool cucumbers make this a refreshing summer salad.

4 servings

For the vinaigrette:

½ CUP SESAME SEEDS

5 TABLESPOONS RICE WINE VINEGAR

2 TABLESPOONS SUGAR

2½ TABLESPOONS SOY SAUCE

PINCH OF CAYENNE

For the salad:

4 CUPS UNSEASONED DASHI *(page 53)* OR WATER

24 LARGE SHRIMP, SHELLED AND DEVEINED

2 MEDIUM CARROTS, PEELED AND CUT INTO JULIENNE (ABOUT 1 CUP)

3 MEDIUM CUCUMBERS, PEELED, SEEDED, AND DICED (ABOUT 2 CUPS)

4 TO 8 SPINACH LEAVES

Roast the sesame seeds in a dry skillet over low heat for 2 or 3 minutes, until they begin to pop and give off a delicious aroma.

Grind the seeds finely in a suribachi or food processor. Add the vinegar, sugar, soy sauce, and cayenne, and mix well. Thin with a tablespoon or two of dashi or water if needed to achieve a pourable consistency.

Heat the dashi to just below a simmer, and poach the shrimp for about 5 minutes, until they turn bright pink. Drain, cover, and refrigerate for at least 30 minutes.

Just before serving, toss the shrimp, carrots, and cucumbers with the sesame vinaigrette. Arrange the salad in mounds on individual plates, and garnish with one or two spinach leaves.

Smoked Salmon Rolls with Daikon Sprouts

Prepare the salmon and sprouts ahead of time, and assemble these rolls at the last minute to preserve their crispness. Serve them on a cedar or black lacquer tray with an assortment of other foods.

10 to 12 rolls

1 POUND SMOKED SALMON, SLICED PAPER THIN

1 CUP DAIKON SPROUTS

1 LEMON

Cut the salmon slices into 2-by-3-inch pieces. Cover and refrigerate.

Wash and dry the sprouts, taking care to eliminate any seeds or yellowed leaves. Separate them into 10 or 12 small bundles. Cover and refrigerate.

Just before serving, juice the lemon. Roll a piece of salmon around each bundle of sprouts, letting the tops of the sprouts peek out of the roll. Sprinkle with the lemon juice and serve.

Avocado and Grapefruit with Shiso

This is an easy salad for summer. The chilled, transparent grapefruit is harmonious with the refreshing tastes of lime and mintlike shiso. Cut-glass serving dishes add to the feeling of freshness.

6 servings

> 1 PINK GRAPEFRUIT
>
> ¼ CUP PLUS 1 TABLESPOON FRESH LIME JUICE
>
> 1 TABLESPOON GRATED LIME ZEST
>
> 1½ TEASPOONS SOY SAUCE
>
> 2 RIPE HAAS AVOCADOS
>
> 6 LARGE SHISO OR MINT LEAVES
>
> NASTURTIUM FLOWERS FOR GARNISH

Peel and section the grapefruit, and remove the membranes and seeds. Cut the fruit into triangular wedges. Cover and chill.

Mix ¼ cup of the lime juice, the zest, and soy sauce in a small bowl.

Just before serving, peel, halve, and pit the avocados. Place the halves, cut side down, on a cutting board, and slice them into wedges the same size as the grapefruit. Sprinkle them with the remaining lime juice to prevent browning.

For each serving, place a shiso leaf on a small plate or bowl. Pile on avocado and grapefruit wedges in overlapping fashion to form a mound. In a deep bowl, the food should come to just below the edge; in a shallow bowl or plate, the arrangement should rise just above the rim. Leave empty space on all sides of the mounded food. Pour the dressing on the side to form a small pool. Garnish with nasturtium flowers.

Jicama, Orange, and Frisée

One early autumn we served this salad for a tea gathering at a San Francisco art gallery. The combination of white jicama, pale green frisée, and orange looked beautiful in small antique Bizen ware bowls, a famous brownish red pottery from Japan.

6 servings

2 ORANGES

3 CUPS LIGHTLY PACKED FRISÉE LEAVES

¼ CUP FRESH LIME JUICE

1 ½ TEASPOONS SOY SAUCE

3 CUPS JULIENNED JICAMA (¾ TO 1 POUND)

1 ½ TABLESPOONS GRATED LIME ZEST

Peel the oranges. Separate them into sections, and remove the seeds and white pulp. Cut the sections into small wedges.

Wash and dry the frisée.

Mix the lime juice and soy sauce in a small bowl.

Divide the frisée among 6 small bowls. Pile the jicama and orange in the center in an overlapping fashion to form a mound. Sprinkle the salad with the lime zest, and pour a scant tablespoon of the dressing on the side of the dish so it forms a pool. Serve immediately.

Sun-Dried Tomatoes with Cucumbers and White Dressing

This light dressing tastes almost like crème fraîche and goes well tossed with green beans, asparagus, or simmered mushrooms, or drizzled over smoked salmon or trout.

4 servings

1 BLOCK (16 OUNCES) SOFT TOFU, PRESSED AND DRAINED *(page 49)*

¼ TEASPOON SALT

2 TABLESPOONS FRESH LEMON JUICE

2 TABLESPOONS SUGAR

½ CUP SUN-DRIED TOMATOES, CUT INTO THIN STRIPS

8 TO 12 FRISÉE LEAVES

2 MEDIUM CUCUMBERS, PEELED AND CUT INTO THIN ROUNDS

FRESHLY GROUND PEPPER

Grind the tofu in a suribachi or a food processor until smooth. Add the salt, lemon juice, and sugar, and mix well.

Soak the tomatoes in hot water for 10 minutes, and drain.

Wash and dry the frisée.

At serving time, toss the cucumbers and tomatoes with the dressing. Arrange the salad in a small mound on each salad plate. Garnish with the greens, and grind a bit of pepper on top.

Apricot and Turnip Salad

For one autumn tea, we hollowed out a persimmon for each guest and filled it with this apricot salad (see Note). If you can find them, pearly white Japanese turnips have an especially mild, sweet taste. Be sure to cut the apricots and turnips into a fine julienne to create a light, delicate appearance. Make the salad a day ahead if you can to let the flavors mature. It keeps in the refrigerator for a week.

4 servings

1 POUND BABY TURNIPS, PEELED

½ TEASPOON SALT

2 OUNCES (⅜ CUP) DRIED APRICOTS

1 TABLESPOON SAKE

2 TABLESPOONS RICE VINEGAR

1 TABLESPOON SUGAR

1 TABLESPOON WATER

PINCH OF SALT

Slice the turnips into the finest matchstick julienne. Toss them with the salt, and let them stand for 5 minutes to draw out any bitterness. Rinse well and drain.

Meanwhile, cut the apricots into a matchstick julienne. Cover them with the sake, and let them stand for 5 minutes. Squeeze them dry.

Mix the vinegar, sugar, water, and salt in a small bowl until the sugar and salt dissolve.

Toss the turnips and apricots with the dressing. Cover and refrigerate for at least an hour, or overnight.

Arrange on individual plates, and serve.

Note:

To serve the salad in Fuyu persimmons or yuzu citrons, cut off one-third of the top of the fruit. Scoop out the flesh, and save for another use. Mound the salad inside, and replace the top to serve.

Recipes

POULTRY AND SEAFOOD

Wind in the Pines Chicken

Tempura Chicken with Asparagus

Miso-Baked Turkey

Duck Seasoned with Sake

Squid with Plum Sauce

Crab Cakes

GRILLED FOODS (YAKIMONO)

Yuan Yaki

    Winter Yuan Sauce

    Warm-Days Yuan Sauce

Chilean Sea Bass Marinated with Sake and Soy, Grilled with Fennel

Grilled Halibut with Shiso Sauce

Glaze-Grilled Salmon with Ginger

Grilled Shrimp or Scallops

Tuna with Sake and Lime

Grilled Matsutake Mushrooms

Grilled Seasonal Vegetables

Poultry, Seafood, and Grilled Foods

Poultry and Seafood

Most of these dishes were created for the Tenshin meal, where tidbits of food are served on a large tray. Two or three thin slices of poultry or seafood are arranged next to a complementary food, such as a chestnut truffle, two wedges of simmered pumpkin, or a tiny mound of cranberry relish, for balance of color, shape, and texture. I've modified the recipes for a Western meal, where the portions are a little more generous.

Wind in the Pines Chicken

The sound of water gently boiling in a kettle is like the sound of wind blowing through pine trees, an image loved by tea enthusiasts. The name for this baked chicken dish comes from the sesame seeds scattered on top as though by a breeze. To serve, stack the chicken squares on platters or skewer them with a pickled cucumber and a shrimp dumpling.

4 servings

1 POUND GROUND CHICKEN OR TURKEY

3 TABLESPOONS SAKE

1 EGG PLUS 2 EGG YOLKS, BEATEN

¼ TEASPOON SALT

2 TABLESPOONS SUGAR

3 TABLESPOONS SOY SAUCE

1 TEASPOON FRESH GINGER JUICE *(page 49)*

For the topping:

1 EGG YOLK, BEATEN

2 TEASPOONS WHITE SESAME SEEDS, LIGHTLY TOASTED

Put half the ground chicken in a skillet with the sake and cook, stirring, over medium heat for about 3 minutes, until the chicken is white. Drain in a colander, and set aside to cool.

Preheat the oven to 350° F. Oil an 8-inch square baking pan with a removable bottom, or line a regular 8-inch square pan with foil, allowing it to extend over two sides.

Mix the rest of the chicken with the egg, yolks, salt, sugar, soy sauce, and ginger juice. Add the cooked chicken and mix well. Spread the chicken mixture evenly in the prepared pan. Bake for 30 minutes, until the chicken is firm in the center.

Remove the chicken from the oven, and immediately brush the top with the beaten egg yolk. The egg will cook and form a glaze. Scatter the sesame seeds over the glaze. When the chicken is cool enough to handle, remove it from the pan, and cut it into 1-inch squares. Serve hot or at room temperature.

Tempura Chicken with Asparagus

Tempura was introduced to Japan in the sixteenth century by the Portuguese, who enjoyed fried shrimp. The Japanese refined the dish by frying shrimp in a light batter. If cooked well, tempura is a delicacy. This dish is perfect for tea gatherings where many different foods are served on a tray, or for the Yakimono dish, when "things cooked over direct heat" are served as a single course in a serving dish that is passed from guest to guest. When the tempura is cut into rounds, a beautiful pattern is revealed.

4 servings

4 BONELESS CHICKEN BREAST HALVES (ABOUT 1 POUND TOTAL)

¼ CUP SAKE

2 TABLESPOONS GINGER JUICE (*page 49*)

12 THIN ASPARAGUS STALKS

2 CUPS FLOUR PLUS MORE FOR DUSTING THE ASPARAGUS

3 TO 4 CUPS CORN OR CANOLA OIL

2 EGG YOLKS

1 CUP ICE WATER

1 CUP ICED PERRIER OR OTHER SPARKLING WATER

Place the chicken breasts between two pieces of wax paper. Use a wooden meat tenderizer or the back of a large knife to flatten them into rectangular shapes roughly 3 by 5 inches. The meat should be quite thin, ¼ to ⅜ inch. Sprinkle the chicken with the sake and ginger juice, and set aside.

Trim the asparagus stalks to the length of the breast halves; roll the asparagus in flour. Wrap each piece of chicken around three stalks; it should go around once and overlap slightly. Try to cover as much of the asparagus as you can. If there are tiny pieces of breast that are extra, use them to patch the roll where needed.

Bring 3 inches of the oil to just under a boil in a large cast iron pot. It's very important that it's as hot as possible, but make sure it doesn't boil, or it will burn and give the food an unpleasant taste.

While the oil is heating, make the tempura batter. Lightly beat the egg yolks in a mixing bowl and stir in the ice water with a fork. Add the 2 cups flour and the iced Perrier. Stir until the ingredients are loosely mixed; the batter should be lumpy. Do not let it stand for long.

When the oil is ready, it shimmers on the surface. Test by throwing a few drops of batter into it. If the batter sizzles and floats to the top, the oil is ready. Oil that is not hot enough will produce soggy tempura.

Dip 2 chicken breast rolls into the batter, and deep fry until golden brown, about 10 minutes, turning several times. Drain on paper towels. Allow the oil to reheat between batches.

When the tempura is slightly cool, cut the rolls into 1½-inch pieces. Arrange them on a platter or tray with the cut side up, and serve at room temperature.

Miso-Baked Turkey

Miso tenderizes the turkey, and its rich flavors mingle with the turkey juices during baking to make a delicate glaze. The miso marinade also partially cooks the meat, resulting in a short baking time. This is a favorite dish for a late-autumn tea gathering. For a beautiful presentation, serve two slices of miso turkey nestled next to a mound of spinach and persimmon on a gleaming black lacquer tray or plate with yellow daikon pickles and bright red Fresh Cranberry Relish *(page 141)*.

4 servings

> 2 CUPS YELLOW SHIRO MISO *(see Glossary, page 189)*
> 2 TABLESPOONS SAKE
> 1 TEASPOON MIRIN
> 1 BONELESS TURKEY BREAST HALF, ABOUT 1½ POUNDS

Mix the miso with the sake and mirin.

Wash the turkey, and pat it dry. Place half the miso mixture in a glass or ceramic baking dish. Roll the turkey in the miso mixture and top it with the remaining half of the miso mixture, covering it completely. Cover the container with plastic wrap, and refrigerate it for 24 hours.

Preheat the oven to 350° F.

Scrape most of the miso mixture from the turkey. Place the turkey in a roasting pan, cover it with foil, and bake for about 20 minutes, until the juices run clear.

Spoon the juices over the breast, and place it under the broiler until nicely browned, about a minute. Let it cool for 30 minutes. Cut it across the grain into thin, diagonal pieces, and serve.

Duck Seasoned with Sake

Duck is a winter food that is marvelous to serve during the holiday season. Here it's simmered and marinated in seasoned sake for a rich, deep flavor.

4 servings

4 BONELESS DUCK BREAST HALVES (ABOUT 1½ POUNDS TOTAL)
1⅓ CUPS DRY SAKE
⅓ CUP SOY SAUCE
¼ CUP MIRIN
¼ TEASPOON RICE VINEGAR

Trim all the visible fat from the duck breasts.

Heat a 12-inch skillet over high heat. Place the duck breasts in the skillet, skin side down, and reduce the heat to medium. Cook the breasts for about 15 minutes, turning once, until the skin is mahogany colored and the fat is rendered out. Spoon the fat from the skillet as the duck cooks, and discard it.

While the duck is cooking, bring a large pot of water to a boil. Combine the sake, soy sauce, mirin, and rice vinegar in a large saucepan, and bring it to a simmer.

When the duck is done, plunge it into the boiling water for a few seconds to remove additional fat.

With chopsticks or tongs, transfer the duck to the simmering sake mixture, and cook it gently for about 8 minutes.

Transfer the duck to a large plate, and set the cooking liquid aside to cool. Pierce the duck at least 10 times with the tip of a metal skewer. Let it rest for 30 minutes.

Skim any fat from the cooled cooking liquid. Return the duck to the liquid, and let it marinate for an hour.

Remove the duck from the marinade, and cut it, across the grain, into thin diagonal slices. Drain it lightly on paper towels, and serve.

Squid with Plum Sauce

This quick and very simple dish looks beautiful served on an amber lacquer tray or plate. The tart red sauce is made from umeboshi, pickled plums available in Oriental markets. The sauce is also delicious on chicken. Make sure you cook the squid only briefly, or it will be tough and chewy.

4 servings

1 POUND SQUID
10 OUNCES UMEBOSHI PLUMS
½ TEASPOON SOY SAUCE

Put a large pot of lightly salted water on to boil.

Cut off the squid's head and tentacles, and discard the head. Rinse the squid well; don't soak it, or it will absorb water. Run your knife along the inside of the body cavity, and slit it so that it lies flat. Cut the body into strips, and cut the tentacles in half crosswise. Plunge the squid into the boiling water, and cook it for about 30 seconds, just until the flesh turns white. Drain it, and set it aside to cool.

Meanwhile, pit the umeboshi plums, and press them through a fine-mesh sieve. Stir in the soy sauce.

Mix the plum sauce with the squid, and serve at room temperature.

Crab Cakes

For a tea gathering, serve these delicate crab cakes on the cedar Hassun tray as the food from the sea. Stack them on the lower left of the tray, and arrange grilled small green peppers (food from the mountain) on the upper right.

6 servings

½ POUND COOKED CRABMEAT

¼ CUP OLIVE OIL

1 LARGE EGG, SLIGHTLY BEATEN

GRATED ZEST 1 LEMON

¼ TEASPOON SALT

CAYENNE

¼ CUP THINLY SLICED GREEN ONIONS

¾ CUP FRESH BREAD CRUMBS

1 TO 2 TABLESPOONS BUTTER

1 TABLESPOON FRESH LEMON JUICE

Pick through the crabmeat to remove any cartilage or bits of shell. Shred the meat into very small pieces.

In a mixing bowl, combine the olive oil, egg, lemon zest, salt, and a couple of pinches of cayenne, mixing well. Stir in the crabmeat and green onions.

Heat the oven to 200° F.

Place the bread crumbs in a shallow dish.

Form the crab mixture into 6 patties, and roll them in the bread crumbs until well coated. (They can be covered and refrigerated at this point for several hours.)

Just before serving, heat the butter in a large sauté pan over medium-high heat. Working in batches if necessary, sauté the crab cakes until golden brown, 1 or 2 minutes per side. Keep them warm in the oven until all the cakes have been cooked.

Sprinkle the crab cakes with lemon juice, and serve.

Grilled Foods (Yakimono)

The Yakimono dish, "things cooked over direct heat," is served alone as the third course of a Chaji meal. The fish, poultry, or seasonal vegetable is typically basted or marinated in sake and soy sauce. Then it is cut into individual portions and threaded onto long metal skewers that reach across a fire pit. Because the seared food doesn't rest on a grill top, its appearance remains natural and beautiful. Its delicate taste and aroma are complemented by aromatic garnishes such as chopped sansho or basil, or grated citron zest.

The exquisite appearance of the grilled food is enhanced by the presentation. Mound the food casually in a distinctive serving dish, allowing enough space around the food so the guests can enjoy the scenery of the dish itself. At a Chaji meal, ceramic handled dishes with interesting shapes and seasonally appropriate decorations are typically used.

A note on charcoal:

Use briquettes that have no petroleum additives to taint the food. Japanese charcoal, available at Japanese hardware and specialty shops, is ideal. It's made from carbonized, chestnut-leaved oak. It has no odor, it burns slowly and very hot, and it doesn't smoke. Alternatively, use slow-burning hardwood chips, such as seasoned oak. Avoid any kind of charcoal or wood that imparts a smoky flavor to the food.

Start the fire about 30 minutes before cooking, and let the coals break up to form thick embers. Never use lighter fluid to start the fire; its kerosene odor will taint the food. Start a few briquettes by setting them on a stove burner over high heat. Watch them carefully. When they are burning well, use tongs to place them in a heat-proof container and transfer them to the grill. Lay the rest of the charcoal on top. Though not traditional, stove-top or gas grills can also be used for these dishes.

Yuan Yaki

Yuan is a marinade of soy, sake, and mirin. Yaki means sauce. Yuan Yaki is the marinade or baste most commonly used for Yakimono foods. It's delicious, and you'll find yourself using it for many other broiled or grilled chicken and fish dishes. As with other foods served during a Kaiseki meal, the strength and style of the Yuan sauce changes with the season. In winter the food is marinated in a strong Yuan sauce; in summer the sauce is lighter, and the food is only basted as it grills.

Winter Yuan Sauce

2½ cups sauce

> 1½ cups soy sauce
> ¾ cup sake
> ½ cup mirin

Stir together the soy sauce, sake, and mirin.

To grill fish:

Prepare a charcoal fire as directed on *page 114*. Wash 1 to 1½ pounds fish fillets, pat them dry, and cut them with the grain into 1½-inch-wide pieces. Pour the sauce over the fish, and refrigerate it for 30 minutes.

Thread each piece of fish onto 2 metal skewers. Insert the skewers against the grain to form a V. (Don't insert them with the grain, or the fish will fall off into the coals.) If the skewers are long enough, each pair can hold 2 or 3 pieces.

Place the skewers on the grill so that they rest on the sides, suspending the fish about 6 inches above the hot coals. Let it cook for 3 or 4 minutes per side, until well browned, brushing it several times with sauce. Test for doneness by twisting the skewers; if they twist easily, the fish is cooked. Remove the skewers and serve the fish.

Warm-Days Yuan Sauce

2½ cups sauce

  1 ½ CUPS SOY SAUCE
  1 CUP SAKE
  A FEW DROPS OF MIRIN

Stir together the soy sauce, sake, and mirin. Use the sauce to baste skewered fish or poultry as it cooks over a charcoal fire.

Chilean Sea Bass Marinated with Sake and Soy, Grilled with Fennel

Thick, juicy Chilean sea bass is perfect for grilling in small pieces. In this dish, Yuan marinade forms a sweet, tangy glaze, and fennel seeds sprinkled on the fire infuse the fish with a hint of anise.

4 to 6 servings

1 ½ POUNDS THICK CHILEAN SEA BASS FILLETS
2 ½ CUPS WINTER YUAN SAUCE *(page 116)*
¼ CUP FENNEL SEEDS

Prepare a charcoal fire as directed on *page 114*. Wash the fish, pat it dry, and cut it with the grain into 1½-inch-wide pieces. Put it in a large glass or ceramic baking dish, cover it with the sauce, and refrigerate it for 30 minutes.

Skewer and grill the fish as directed on *page 116,* sprinkling the fennel seeds on the coals just before you place the skewers on the grill.

Grilled Halibut with Shiso Sauce

Shiso is an aromatic herb with a bright, mysterious taste reminiscent of mint and cinnamon. Here it's mixed with a rice vinegar–sake sauce. Serve the sauce in a tiny spouted container; only a teaspoon or two is needed for each serving.

4 to 6 servings

1½ POUNDS HALIBUT OR OTHER WHITE FISH FILLETS
SALT
10 SHISO LEAVES, STEMS REMOVED
2 TABLESPOONS RICE VINEGAR
1½ TABLESPOONS SAKE

Prepare a charcoal fire as directed on *page 114*. Wash the fish, pat it dry, and cut it with the grain into 1½-inch-wide pieces. Salt it lightly on both sides.

Wash the shiso leaves, and pat them dry. Grind them into a paste with a suribachi or a mortar and pestle. Add the rice vinegar and sake, and mix well.

Skewer and grill the fish as directed on *page 116*.

Mound the cooked fish in the center of a large serving dish. Strain the rice vinegar sauce into a spouted container, and pass with the fish.

Glaze-Grilled Salmon with Ginger

Serve salmon in the spring when it's at its best, lean and delicately flavored. Its deep red flesh looks especially beautiful served in blue-and-white porcelain or rough, wabi-style unglazed pottery.

4 to 6 servings

> 1 ½ POUNDS SALMON FILLETS
>
> SALT
>
> 3 TABLESPOONS SOY SAUCE
>
> 3 TABLESPOONS MIRIN
>
> ½ TABLESPOON SUGAR
>
> 2 TEASPOONS GINGER JUICE *(page 49)*

Prepare a charcoal fire as directed on *page 114*.

Wash the fish, pat it dry, and sprinkle it with salt. Refrigerate it for 30 minutes.

Meanwhile, heat the soy sauce, mirin, and sugar in a small saucepan over medium heat until the sugar dissolves. When the mixture has cooled, add the ginger juice.

Cut the fish into strips about 1 by 2 inches, and skewer it as directed on *page 116*. Brush it all over with the sauce, and grill it as directed on *page 116*, basting it several times.

Remove the fish from the skewers, and serve immediately.

Grilled Shrimp or Scallops

For an early-morning summer tea, one or two grilled shrimp or scallops are arranged on a tray with a tiny mound of Vinegared Avocado *(page 135)* and cucumber pickles. For a more formal Chaji meal, the seafood is stacked on a cedar Hassun tray and served with sake.

4 servings

1 POUND LARGE, SHELLED, AND DEVEINED SHRIMP OR 1 POUND SEA
    SCALLOPS
2½ CUPS WARM-DAYS YUAN SAUCE *(page 117)*
4 OR 5 FRESH BASIL LEAVES, CHOPPED

Wash the shellfish, pat them dry, and thread them onto skewers.

Heat the sauce in a small saucepan over medium heat until it thickens slightly.

Prepare a charcoal fire as directed on *page 114* or heat the broiler.

Brush the shellfish all over with the sauce. Grill or broil them about 6 inches from the heat, basting several times, until they are just cooked, about 2 minutes per side.

Arrange the shellfish in a casual pile on a plate. Garnish with the basil, and serve.

Tuna with Sake and Lime

Tuna is tricky to cook well. The secret is to grill it fast, close to the fire. Serve this summer dish on blue-and-white porcelain to convey a cool feeling.

4 to 6 servings

1½ POUNDS TUNA FILLET

4 TABLESPOONS SAKE

4 TABLESPOONS FRESH LIME JUICE

2 TEASPOONS GRATED LIME ZEST

2 TABLESPOONS SOY SAUCE

Wash the fish and pat it dry. Cut it with the grain into 1½-inch-wide slices. Combine the sake, lime juice, lime zest, and soy sauce. Pour this marinade over the fish, and refrigerate it for 30 minutes.

Prepare a charcoal fire as directed on *page 114*. Skewer the fish as directed on *page 116*. Rest the skewers on the side of the grill so the fish is suspended about 4 inches above the fire. Cook it for 2 to 3 minutes per side, brushing several times with the marinade, until it's brown all over. Test for doneness by wiggling a skewer; it will move freely when the fish is done. Remove the tuna from the skewers, and serve immediately.

Grilled Matsutake Mushrooms

Matsutake, or pine mushrooms, are a great delicacy in Japan, where they grow only in the wild in red pine forests. They are very expensive, and until recently were difficult to find in the United States. They are now being harvested in the forests of northern California and Oregon. These large mushrooms with tight caps have a wonderful pinewoods aroma. Never wash them; just wipe them with a damp paper towel. Don't overcook; the fresh, woodsy flavor is one of their delights. Other large wild mushrooms such as shiitake or chanterelle may be substituted.

4 servings

4 MATSUTAKE MUSHROOMS, ½ TO 1 POUND
4 TEASPOONS SOY SAUCE
4 TEASPOONS YUZU OR LEMON JUICE

Prepare a charcoal fire as directed on *page 114* or preheat the broiler. Position the grill or rack about 4 inches from the heat.

Trim ½ inch from the mushroom stems. Cut each mushroom in half. If using the broiler, brush them lightly with vegetable oil.

Grill or broil for about 5 minutes, turning occasionally, until just tender. Set them aside to cool slightly.

Meanwhile, mix the soy sauce and citrus juice.

Tear the mushrooms lengthwise into small pieces. Mound them in small, individual bowls, top with the soy dressing, and serve immediately.

Grilled Seasonal Vegetables

Potatoes, sweet potatoes, carrots, baby beets, and artichokes all taste wonderful grilled. At an early-spring tea, one kind of grilled vegetable is served as the Yakimono dish, with enough pieces so that each guest has one. Sansho or basil leaves add a piquant touch to the dish.

4 servings

1 POUND SEASONAL VEGETABLES
¼ CUP SAKE
¼ CUP MIRIN
¼ CUP SOY SAUCE
¼ CUP MINCED SANSHO OR BASIL LEAVES

Prepare a charcoal fire as directed on *page 114*.

Peel vegetables that have tough outer skins. Cut them into 1-inch pieces, and slide the pieces onto metal skewers.

Heat the sake, mirin, and soy sauce in a small saucepan over medium heat, and simmer for a minute or two until slightly thickened.

Brush the skewered vegetables with the sauce. Grill, about 6 inches from the fire, turning and basting, until the pieces are browned and feel tender when pricked with a bamboo skewer.

Slide the vegetables off the skewers, and mound the pieces on a platter. Sprinkle them with the minced sansho, and serve.

Recipes

Vegetable Dishes, Rice, and Pickles

Vegetables

One of the delights of the Kaiseki meal is the serving of newly harvested vegetables from local farms and gardens. Baby turnips are delicious in soups; mustard greens brighten the assortment of foods served on trays; sweet potatoes and teriyaki walnuts complement the taste of sake. Seasonal and adaptable, the recipes that follow will grace your table at almost any meal.

Spinach and Fuyu Persimmon with Sesame

The deep green of the spinach and the pale orange of the persimmon, reflect the autumn leaves scattered by wind. Serve this when persimmons first appear in the markets in November.

4 servings

2 POUNDS SPINACH

½ CUP TAHINI (SESAME PASTE)

¼ CUP SAKE

¼ CUP UNSEASONED DASHI (*page 53*) OR WATER

1 TABLESPOON SOY SAUCE

2 SMALL FUYU PERSIMMONS

Steam the spinach until it just begins to wilt. Drain it and set it aside to cool.

Spread about a quarter of the spinach in a strip across a bamboo rolling mat, about 2 inches from the bottom. Fold the bottom of the mat over the spinach, and roll away from you, pressing firmly. When you come to the end of the roll, twist it over the sink to squeeze out all liquid. Press the roll back into shape, and unroll it. Cut the rolled spinach into 1-inch pieces, and transfer them to a mixing bowl. Repeat with the remaining spinach, and set aside.

Stir together the tahini, sake, dashi, and soy sauce until well blended.

Peel the persimmons, and cut them into ½-inch cubes. Cover them with cold water to prevent discoloring.

Just before serving, drain the persimmons. Toss them with the spinach and enough sesame dressing to evenly coat the ingredients. Serve mounded in individual dishes or arranged with other foods on a large plate or tray.

Turnips with Miso Walnut Sauce

The Japanese love to serve turnips in delicate broths or topped with this golden sauce fragrant with lemon zest. Use the best white miso you can find.

4 servings

8 (2-INCH) BABY TURNIPS WITH LEAFY TOPS
6 TO 8 CUPS PLUS 2 TABLESPOONS UNSEASONED DASHI *(page 53)*
½ CUP WHITE MISO
1 TABLESPOON SUGAR
3 TABLESPOONS MIRIN
1 EGG YOLK
2 TABLESPOONS FINELY CHOPPED WALNUTS
1 TABLESPOON LEMON ZEST

Trim all but 1½ inches of the greens from the turnips, and save them for another use. Cut off the top of each turnip one-fourth of the way down, and set it aside. Scoop a small well out of the bottom to hold the sauce.

Heat all but 2 tablespoons of the dashi in a large saucepan to just below a simmer. Gently cook the turnips until just tender; the bottoms will take about 10 minutes and the tops a little less. Drain and set aside.

In a small saucepan, combine the miso, sugar, mirin, the remaining 2 tablespoons dashi, and the egg yolk. Cook over low heat, stirring, for about 5 minutes, until the sugar dissolves and the sauce is glossy. Stir in the walnuts.

For each serving, place a turnip bottom in a small dish. Spoon sauce into the well, letting it spill over just a bit. Place a turnip top at an angle next to the bottom. Sprinkle with the lemon zest, and serve.

Simmered Shiitake Mushrooms

The Japanese have been cultivating shiitake mushrooms for centuries, and use them in many dishes. Simmered dry shiitakes are delicious in Nimono soups; sliced thinly and rolled in sushi; or served as an accompaniment on trays with rice, pickles, and other delicacies.

4 servings

8 MEDIUM DRIED SHIITAKE MUSHROOMS
1 CUP UNSEASONED DASHI *(page 53)*
1 TABLESPOON SOY SAUCE
PINCH OF SUGAR
PINCH OF SALT
1 TEASPOON SAKE

Soak the mushrooms in cold water to cover until soft, at least 30 minutes. Drain them, reserving ½ cup of the liquid.

Discard the mushroom stems, and place the caps in a saucepan with the dashi, reserved mushroom liquid, soy sauce, sugar, salt, and sake. Heat to just below a simmer, and cook for about 30 minutes, until well cooked and seasoned.

Mustard Greens with Sesame Dressing

This is one of my favorite ways to prepare mustard greens. For a tea, serve them in a black lacquer box with gleaming black beans and steamed carrots cut in plum blossom shapes. Try the sauce in summer with tender green beans or tiny cherry tomatoes.

4 servings

½ CUP WHITE SESAME SEEDS

2 TABLESPOONS SOY SAUCE

2 TABLESPOONS SAKE

1 TABLESPOON MIRIN

ABOUT 2 TABLESPOONS UNSEASONED DASHI *(page 53)* OR WATER

1 POUND MUSTARD GREENS

Toast the sesame seeds in a dry skillet over low heat, stirring, just until they begin to pop and give off a wonderful aroma.

Grind them into a paste in a suribachi or food processor. Mix in the soy sauce, sake, and mirin. Thin with enough dashi or water to create a thick dressing.

Carefully wash the mustard greens. Steam them in a large pot for 5 to 8 minutes, until just tender. Drain and cool.

Spread about half the greens in a strip across a bamboo rolling mat, about 2 inches from the bottom. Fold the bottom of the mat over the greens and roll away from you, pressing firmly. When you come to the end of the roll, twist it over the sink to squeeze out all liquid. Press the roll back into shape, and unroll it. Cut the rolled greens into 1-inch pieces, and transfer them to a mixing bowl. Repeat with the remaining greens.

Toss the rolled greens with the sesame dressing. Serve at room temperature.

Variation:

Substitute spinach for the mustard greens; it will melt in your mouth.

Pine Nut Dressing

This wonderful dressing goes well with all sorts of cooked greens. In autumn, toss it with chrysanthemum leaves for a tea gathering that celebrates the Chrysanthemum Festival.

About 1 cup

1 CUP PINE NUTS

4 TABLESPOONS UNSEASONED DASHI *(page 53)* OR WATER

2½ TEASPOONS USUKUCHI (LIGHT) SOY SAUCE

1 TABLESPOON SAKE

Toast the pine nuts in a dry skillet over low heat, stirring, just until they're lightly browned and fragrant. Be careful; they burn easily.

Grind them into a paste in a suribachi or food processor. Mix in the dashi, soy sauce, and sake.

Yellow Finn Potatoes with Ginger

I look forward to the fall harvest of Yellow Finn potatoes. Their delicate taste is perfect for simmering with ginger. In this dish, their octagonal shapes look beautiful clustered in a black lacquer box next to bright orange carrots and white daikon pickles.

4 to 6 servings

> 1 POUND YELLOW FINN POTATOES (10 TO 12 SMALL POTATOES)
> 1 (2-INCH) PIECE FRESH GINGER, PEELED AND CUT INTO ⅛-INCH SLICES
> 4 CUPS UNSEASONED DASHI *(page 53)*
> 1 TEASPOON USUKUCHI (LIGHT) SOY SAUCE

Use a small paring knife to trim the ends of each potato, and then peel down its length in one movement. Trim the rest of the potato in the same way to create an octagonal shape. It doesn't have to be an exact octagon; what's important is the smoothness of each side. Trim off a bit of the flesh if necessary to create a pleasing shape. Place the potatoes in cold water as you peel them to prevent discoloration.

Drain the potatoes, and place them in a saucepan with the ginger, dashi, and soy sauce. Bring to a simmer, and cook gently until the potatoes are barely tender, 10 to 15 minutes. Don't let the mixture boil, or it will turn bitter.

Let the potatoes cool in the broth. Cover the saucepan, refrigerate, and let the potatoes marinate overnight. Just before serving, drain the potatoes, and remove the ginger.

Kabocha Pumpkin

Small, sweet Kabocha and Hokkaido pumpkins are wonderful as the main ingredient in soups or simmered in wedges and served in a decorative dish. Kabocha have a beautifully patterned green skin and bright orange flesh that reflect late-fall colors.

6 servings

> 1 POUND KABOCHA OR HOKKAIDO PUMPKIN
>
> 1 CUP UNSEASONED DASHI *(page 53)*
>
> 1½ CUPS WATER
>
> 5 TABLESPOONS SUGAR
>
> 1 TEASPOON SALT

Cut the pumpkin in half. Scoop out and discard the seeds and fibrous pulp. Cut it into quarters and then into wedges about 2 inches long and 1 inch wide. With a sharp paring knife, remove most of the green peel, leaving a little rind in a camouflage-like pattern of bits and stripes. The slight peel will keep the pumpkin from disintegrating as it simmers.

Combine the dashi, water, sugar, and salt in a saucepan, stirring until the sugar dissolves. Add the pumpkin, and heat to just below a simmer. Cook gently for about 15 minutes, until the pumpkin is almost soft.

Transfer the pumpkin and cooking liquid to a glass dish. Cover and refrigerate it for about 2 hours. Drain the pumpkin and allow it to return to room temperature before serving. For each serving, arrange 2 wedges on a small tray or dish, one skin side up, the other skin side down.

Vinegared Avocado

Ripe avocados need very little to enhance their luscious flavor. Simply peel and pit an avocado, and cut it into wedges. Place it in a beautiful bowl that complements its pale green color, and drizzle it lightly with the best-quality rice vinegar.

Asparagus with Walnut Dressing

This tangy walnut dressing is delicate enough not to overshadow the taste of the asparagus. (It also goes well with steamed spinach.) Serve this springtime dish in individual bowls or plates that complement the color and shape of the asparagus.

4 servings

½ CUP WALNUTS
¼ CUP SOY SAUCE
1 TABLESPOON SUGAR
1 TABLESPOON SAKE
1 POUND ASPARAGUS

Crush the walnuts in a food processor or suribachi, leaving small chunks. Add the soy sauce, sugar, and sake, and blend for 5 or 10 seconds, just until well combined.

Trim and discard the woody bottom portions of the asparagus stalks. Cut them into 1¾-inch pieces. Steam the asparagus for no longer that 2 minutes. You'll know it's perfectly cooked when you smell its faint aroma escaping from the steamer. Rinse it with cold water and drain.

For each serving, arrange stems and tips in a mound, with tips aiming upward. Drizzle with the dressing, and serve.

Tofu, Corn, and Baby Green Beans

Bright green and yellow specks tantalize the eye in this sushilike summer dish. Feel free to make it with any fresh, seasonal vegetables. Always consider how the colors and flavors come together. In winter, try it with Simmered Shiitake Mushrooms *(page 130)* and finely julienned carrots.

6 to 8 servings

> 1 BLOCK (12 OUNCES) FIRM TOFU, RINSED AND PRESSED *(page 49)*
> 1 TEASPOON ALL-PURPOSE FLOUR
> ½ TEASPOON SALT
> 1 TABLESPOON SUGAR
> 1 TEASPOON SAKE
> ¾ CUP FRESH CORN KERNELS (ABOUT 1 EAR)
> ¾ CUP CHOPPED BABY GREEN BEANS

Mash the tofu in a suribachi or with a fork until smooth. Add the flour, salt, sugar, and sake, mixing well. Fold in the corn and green beans.

Dampen 2 clean tea towels and 2 bamboo rollers. Place one roller on top of one of the towels. Spread half the tofu mixture in a strip across the roller about 2 inches from the bottom. Fold the bottom of the roller and the towel up over the tofu and roll away from you, pressing firmly. Press to shape the roll. Repeat with the remaining tofu mixture and the other towel and roller.

Put the tofu rolls, still in the rollers, in a large steamer, laying them flat. Steam for 15 minutes, and set them aside to cool.

Unroll the rollers and the towels. Cut the tofu rolls into 3 or 4 pieces, each about 3 inches long. Slice each piece in half on the diagonal, leaving ¾ inch on either end.

For each serving, arrange 2 pieces on a small plate so they are sitting on their bases with the diagonal side up.

VEGETABLE DISHES, RICE, AND PICKLES

Sweet Black Beans

These large black soybeans are a traditional New Year's food, usually served piled next to bright orange carrots and white radishes cut in blossom shapes. The "rusty nail" method is the secret that imparts a delightful and mysterious flavor. Black soybeans are called kuromame in Asian markets.

4 servings

    1 CUP BLACK SOYBEANS

    6 CUPS COLD WATER

    ½ CUP SUGAR

    ½ TEASPOON SALT

    ½ TEASPOON BAKING SODA

    ¼ CUP SOY SAUCE

    2 (2-INCH) NAILS IN A SMALL CLOTH BAG

Sort through the beans, discarding any stones or broken beans. Place them in a large pot with 5 cups of the water and the sugar, salt, baking soda, soy sauce, and nails. Soak overnight.

Bring the beans to a boil, and add ½ cup cold water. When they come back to a boil, add the remaining ½ cup water. When they come to a boil the third time, turn down the heat, and simmer. Float a small wooden lid over the beans to keep them submerged. Cook them for 3 or 4 hours, until soft but not mushy. Add more water if needed.

Drain the beans, reserving the cooking liquid, and remove the bag of nails. Serve the beans at room temperature as a complement to colorful foods. Any leftover beans can be refrigerated in the cooking liquid for 3 or 4 days; the flavor just gets better.

Chestnut Puree

I relish the smell of chestnuts roasting in city streets and cooking in our kitchens for early-winter tea gatherings. It's not easy to peel chestnuts, but it's well worth the trouble. In Western cuisine, they are wonderful pureed with celery, a good bouillon, and lots of butter and cream. For a Kaiseki meal, we keep it simple, just adding a delicate broth and a bit of sake. The cooked, pureed chestnuts are twisted into truffle shapes using a tea towel.

4 to 6 servings (about 10 truffles)

1 POUND WHOLE CHESTNUTS
5 CUPS UNSEASONED DASHI *(page 53)*
2 TEASPOONS SAKE
PINCH OF SALT
1 TEASPOON SUGAR

With a small, sharp knife, cut the chestnuts in half and peel off the outer and inside skin. Be patient; it will take quite a while.

Place the peeled chestnuts in a large saucepan with the dashi, sake, salt, and sugar. Heat to just below a simmer. Cook gently for about 45 minutes, until the chestnuts are soft.

Drain the chestnuts, and puree them in a suribachi or food processor.

When the puree is cool enough to handle, dampen and squeeze out a tea towel, and spread it open in one hand. With the other hand, scoop a large tablespoonful of puree into the center of the towel. Gently wrap the towel around the puree, and twist the top of the towel to form a rounded shape. (It should be about 1½ inches in diameter, and will have swirl marks from the folds of the towel.) Unwrap the towel, set the finished chestnut truffle aside, and repeat with the rest of the puree.

To serve, place 1 or 2 chestnut truffles on a small tray or plate with colorful autumn foods.

Teriyaki Walnuts

Teriyaki is a sweet soy sauce glaze that's often used for fish or chicken. These savory, teriyaki-toasted walnuts can be served for tea on the Hassun tray as food from the mountains.

4 to 6 servings (about 2 cups)

2 CUPS WALNUT HALVES

3 TABLESPOONS SOY SAUCE

2 TABLESPOONS SAKE

1 TABLESPOON SESAME OIL

1 TEASPOON GROUND POWDERED GINGER

PINCH OF CAYENNE

1 TABLESPOON DARK BROWN SUGAR

1 TABLESPOON WHITE SESAME SEEDS

SALT *(optional)*

Preheat the oven to 325° F. Line a jelly-roll pan and a large plate with foil. Put the walnuts in a mixing bowl.

Mix the soy sauce, sake, sesame oil, ginger, cayenne, brown sugar, and sesame seeds in a small saucepan. Cook over medium heat, stirring, until the sugar is dissolved.

Pour the soy sauce mixture over the walnuts, and toss to coat. Spread the nuts in the prepared pan, and bake for about 15 minutes, until lightly browned.

Spread the nuts on the prepared plate to cool. Taste them, and sprinkle with salt if needed. Serve within 2 hours or store in an airtight container to prevent sogginess.

Fresh Cranberry Relish

This uncooked relish has a pleasing crunch. For a November tea gathering with a Thanksgiving theme, serve it in a small mound next to slices of Miso-Baked Turkey *(page 108)*.

10 to 12 servings

12 OUNCES FRESH CRANBERRIES
¼ CUP SUGAR

Wash and drain the cranberries, discarding any soft or discolored ones. Chop them coarsely by hand. Transfer the cranberries to a glass bowl, and stir in the sugar. Cover with plastic wrap and let them sit at room temperature overnight.

Sweet Potatoes with Black Sesame Seeds

These simple, elegant sweet potatoes were the mountain food served on the Hassun tray at an autumn tea gathering. Black sesame seeds are easy to find in Oriental markets.

4 to 6 servings

> 2 LARGE SWEET POTATOES (ABOUT 1 POUND)
> ½ CUP BLACK SESAME SEEDS

Scrub the sweet potatoes, and slice them into ½-inch rounds, leaving the peel on. Cook them in lightly salted water for about 10 minutes, until tender but still holding their shape. Drain and set aside.

Toast the sesame seeds in a dry skillet over low heat for 2 or 3 minutes, until they begin to pop and give off a delicious aroma.

Scatter the seeds evenly and sparsely over the flat sides of the sweet potato slices. Stack the slices in mounds on small trays or serving plates.

Lotus Root Chips

These quick and easy chips are a wonder to look at and a delight to eat. Lotus roots are patterned with hollow tubes that run up and down their length. When thinly sliced and deep-fried, they look like snowflakes. Serve them as the mountain food on the Hassun tray or as a garnish for your main course. Fresh lotus root is in season in the late fall and winter, and is easy to find in Asian markets.

4 servings

RICE VINEGAR
½ POUND LOTUS ROOT
CANOLA OR CORN OIL
SALT

Pour a little vinegar in a bowl of water.

Peel the lotus root, trim the ends, and place it immediately in the acidulated water to prevent discoloration. Slice the root into ⅛-inch rounds, trimming and discarding any blackened parts. Return the slices to the water.

Heat 4 inches of oil in a large cast iron pot to just below a boil. Don't let it burn, or it will give the food an unpleasant taste. When ready, the oil will shimmer. Throw a few drops of water into it; if the water forms balls and sizzles, you can begin frying.

Pat 4 or 5 lotus root slices dry, and fry them, turning, until lightly browned, about 5 minutes. Drain them on paper towels, and allow the oil to reheat between batches. If it's not hot enough, the chips will be greasy.

Lightly salt the chips. Serve them within 4 hours to avoid sogginess.

Noodles with Ginger

The week before New Year's is a wonderful time to share a bowl of tea with friends and reflect on the passing year. Tea bowls with zodiac signs of past and future years spark conversation. In addition to tea and sweets, these highly seasoned buckwheat noodles are served to ensure good fortune and long life. They are best with freshly made soba noodles, which you can often buy at Japanese noodle restaurants, especially at New Year's time, but packaged soba noodles are fine.

4 to 6 servings

6 CUPS UNSEASONED DASHI *(page 53)*

1½ TABLESPOONS SUGAR

4 TABLESPOONS SAKE

3½ TABLESPOONS SOY SAUCE

¼ TEASPOON SALT

4 TO 5 INCHES FRESH GINGER, PEELED

1½ POUNDS FRESH OR PACKAGED SOBA NOODLES

Bring a large pot of lightly salted water to a boil for the noodles.

Meanwhile, combine the dashi with the sugar, sake, soy sauce, and salt in a large saucepan. Heat it to just below a simmer; make sure it never boils.

Meanwhile, grate the ginger.

Cook the noodles in the boiling water for about 3 minutes. (Packaged soba will take a little longer.)

Drain the noodles and divide them among large individual soup or noodle bowls. Add enough hot broth to just reach the top of the noodles. Depending on how strong you like your ginger, place a teaspoon or two on top of each portion and serve immediately. Let your guests mix the ginger with the broth.

Rice

Rice is served four times during the formal Kaiseki meal. First, a thin line of white rice, just enough for three bites, is served with miso soup to stimulate the appetite. The rice is never flavored, yet it is absolutely delicious.

The second serving comes after the guests have drunk a few sips of sake with the mukozuke. The rice is scooped in individual portions and served mounded in a black lacquer dish. The third rice comes much later, after the main courses have been served. This time the guests help themselves to as much as they want.

The rice continues to cook on the stove during the meal. A crust eventually forms on the bottom of the pot, and this is broken into pieces and mixed with hot water and a pinch of salt. It's served at the end of the meal in a spouted lacquer dish with a ladle. Pickles accompany this last rice to clean the palate for the tea and sweets to follow.

Rice is central to the informal tea gathering called Tenshin Chakai. Tidbits of food are arranged on a tray, and the rice is formed into seasonal shapes: a flower blossom in spring, a gourd in autumn, a fan in summer. The rice may be cooked with seasonal foods; chestnuts, adzuki beans, and sweet potatoes make beautiful patterns and colors mixed with the pure white grains. Squares of rice may be dusted with minced green shiso leaves or sprinkled with black sesame seeds. Round shapes of rice are mixed with fresh-shelled green peas or strips of bright red umeboshi plums. For New Year's, strips of gold leaf are gently pressed on top of diamond-shaped rice for good luck.

White Rice

Look for the best-quality short-grain Japanese rice harvested in autumn; it's stickier than long-grain rice, which is not a substitute. Ask the grocer at your Oriental market what brand he or she recommends.

8 servings

4 CUPS SHORT-GRAIN JAPANESE WHITE RICE

4⅛ CUPS WATER

1 TABLESPOON SAKE

PINCH OF SALT

Wash the rice by gently swishing it in a bowl of cold water. Drain and repeat two or three times, until the water is clear. Let the rice rest in a colander for 45 minutes.

Put the rice, water, sake, and salt in a heavy-bottomed pot with a tight lid. Bring it to a boil. When steam begins to escape, immediately turn the heat to low, and simmer for 40 minutes.

For Kaiseki, use a dampened bamboo paddle to press down the outer edges of the cooked rice while it's still in the pot. When it's firm around the edges, scoop 1½ inches down at the edge of the pot. Lift up and tilt the paddle away from you into a black lacquer rice bowl. Use another damp paddle to guide the rice into the bowl with the cut edge facing up. This makes a beautiful line of white in the bowl. Put the lids on the rice bowls, and serve immediately.

Rice with Chestnuts

This rice is prepared with the first chestnuts of the fall and pressed into gourd shapes. Gourds are favored in the tea room. A famous Zen painting shows a monk fishing for an elusive catfish with a narrow-necked gourd—a paradoxical task. Certain ceramic tea caddies are referred to as "gourd-shaped," and a large dried gourd is used in winter to hold charcoal.

8 servings

10 TO 15 FRESH CHESTNUTS

4 CUPS SHORT-GRAIN JAPANESE WHITE RICE

4½ CUPS WATER

½ CUP SAKE

½ TEASPOON SALT

With a small, sharp knife, cut the chestnuts in half, and peel off the outer and inner skin. Be patient; it will take some time. Place the peeled nuts in a bowl of cold water.

Wash the rice by gently swishing it in a bowl of cold water. Drain and repeat two or three times, until the water is clear. Let the rice rest in a colander for 45 minutes.

Drain the chestnuts, and put them in a heavy-bottomed pot with a tight-fitting lid. Add the rice, water, sake, and salt. Bring the mixture to a boil. When steam begins to escape, immediately turn the heat to low, and simmer for 40 minutes.

Remove the pot from the heat, and stir to combine the rice and chestnuts. When the rice is cool enough to handle, use a rice mold *(page 49)* to form it into shapes. Serve at room temperature.

Rice with Sweet Potato

Cooked with tiny chunks of pale yellow sweet potato, this rice is molded into chrysanthemum flower shapes for an early-autumn tea celebrating the Chrysanthemum Festival.

8 servings

1 MEDIUM SWEET POTATO
4 CUPS SHORT-GRAIN JAPANESE WHITE RICE
4½ CUPS WATER
½ CUP SAKE
½ TEASPOON SALT

Peel and cube the sweet potato, and cover it with cold water to prevent discoloration.

Wash the rice by gently swishing it in a bowl of cold water. Drain and repeat two or three times, until the water is clear. Let the rice rest in a colander for 45 minutes.

Drain the sweet potato, and put it in a heavy-bottomed pot with a tight-fitting lid. Add the rice, water, sake, and salt. Bring it to a boil. When steam begins to escape, immediately turn the heat to low, and simmer for 40 minutes.

Remove the pot from the heat, and stir to combine the rice and sweet potato. When the mixture is cool enough to handle, use a rice mold (*page 49*) to form it into the desired shapes. Serve at room temperature.

Shiso Rice

Shredded shiso, a green, mintlike herb, looks beautiful with the white rice, and infuses it with a refreshing taste for a summer meal. If shiso is not available, substitute fresh basil or cilantro.

8 servings

4 CUPS SHORT-GRAIN JAPANESE WHITE RICE
4⅛ CUPS WATER
1 TABLESPOON SAKE
PINCH OF SALT
4 SMALL SHISO LEAVES

Wash the rice by gently swishing it in a bowl of cold water. Drain and repeat two or three times, until the water is clear. Let the rice rest in a colander for 45 minutes.

Put the rice, water, sake, and salt in a heavy-bottomed pot with a tight-fitting lid. Bring it to a boil. When steam begins to escape, immediately turn the heat to low, and simmer for 40 minutes.

Remove the rice from the heat, and let it stand, covered, for 10 minutes. Wash the shiso leaves and pat them dry. Discard the stems, and cut the leaves into short shreds.

Stir the shiso into the rice, and use a rice mold *(page 49)* to form it into the desired shapes.

Sushi Rice

The trick to making sticky sushi rice is to cool it quickly while mixing in the mirin and vinegar. It's a good idea to enlist a friend to help fan the rice.

4 cups

    2 CUPS SHORT-GRAIN JAPANESE WHITE RICE
    2½ CUPS WATER
    ⅓ CUP MIRIN
    3 TABLESPOONS RICE VINEGAR
    ½ TEASPOON SALT

Wash the rice by gently swishing it in a bowl of cold water. Drain and repeat two or three times, until the water is clear. Let the rice rest in a colander for 45 minutes.

Put the rice and water in a heavy-bottomed pot with a tight-fitting lid. Bring it to a boil. When steam begins to escape, immediately turn the heat to low, and simmer for 40 minutes.

Remove the rice from the heat, and let it stand, covered, for 10 minutes.

In the meantime, heat the mirin, vinegar, and salt in a small saucepan until the salt dissolves.

Put the cooked rice in a large mixing bowl. While vigorously fanning the rice, slowly stir in the mirin mixture. Continue stirring and fanning until the rice is cool. Use it to make sushi as directed in the next recipe.

Nori Maki Sushi

Nori maki is a general term for sushi rolled in seaweed, and it is a delightful food to serve at the informal meal called Tenshin Chakai, where tidbits of food are arranged on a tray. Traditional sushi is made with vinegared rice and fresh, raw seafood, but other fillings are delicious too. Here are just some of the ingredients you can choose:

Simmered Shiitake Mushrooms (page 130)
Peeled and seeded cucumber
Takuan (daikon pickle)
Avocado
Shiso leaves
Black sesame seeds
Chopped cooked shrimp

4 to 6 servings (8 rolls)

YOUR CHOICE OF 2 OR 3 INGREDIENTS LISTED ABOVE
8 SHEETS NORI
4 CUPS SUSHI RICE *(page 151)*

Cut selected ingredients into ¼-inch-wide julienne; you will need 3 or 4 strips per roll. (Allow 1 teaspoon black sesame seeds and 2 or 3 shrimp per roll.)

Toast the nori by holding it a few inches from a hot burner just until it turns green-gold.

Place a sheet of toasted nori, shiny side down, on a bamboo rolling mat, lining up the bottoms of the nori and mat. With a wooden spoon, spread a ½-inch-thick layer of sushi rice over the nori, leaving a 1-inch border on the bottom and a 2-inch border at the top. You will need about ½ cup rice.

Starting 2 inches from the bottom of the rice, spread the cucumber and other ingredients in a 1-inch-wide strip across the rice.

Using the roller, fold the bottom of the nori over the filling. Continue rolling away from you, pressing firmly with the roller. When you come to the end, press to shape the roll, and unroll the sushi. The roll should be no more than 2 inches in diameter. Repeat with the remaining sheets of nori.

Wet a very sharp knife, and cut the rolls into 1-inch pieces. Arrange them on a plate or tray with cut sides up.

Pickles

Crisp and sour, tart and tangy, pickles have been made in every part of the world for thousands of years. Long before refrigeration, pickling was one of the best ways to preserve food. Every region of Japan has a celebrated kind of pickle. Freshness, crispness, and an endless variety of delicate and strong flavors characterize pickles made from Chinese cabbage, daikon, ginger, greens, cucumber, eggplant, and plums.

In Japanese, pickles are called konomono, which means "a thing for incense." Incense contests were a popular pastime among tenth-century Japanese nobles. Incense was made by blending fragrant woods, roots, leaves, and flowers with ground seashells, cloves, camphor, star anise, and cinnamon. These ingredients were bound with honey and charcoal dust, were kneaded into small nuggets, and were roasted over charcoal fires. Prizes were awarded for the most pleasing and complex fragrances. A courtier judging an incense contest would chew a few slices of pickled daikon to keep his sense of smell sharp.

In Kaiseki cuisine, three to five types of pickles are served with the last portion of rice to clean the palate before the sweets and green tea. Takuan, a bright yellow pickled daikon, is cut into rectangles. Other pickles are chosen according to their color and the season. They are cut into contrasting shapes, and arranged together in a distinctive bowl.

I've included traditional Japanese pickle recipes that are easy to make. The chrysanthemum pickles are my favorite; ginger blossom pickles are a pleasure to serve because they are so unusual. I've also included recipes for some American pickles that are suitable for a tea gathering. They require a hot-water-bath method of processing, which the Japanese don't use but is good to know. While making these pickles, you can "put up" some of your favorite seasonal fruits at the same time.

No matter which method you use, choose the freshest, best-quality ingredients. Pickle fresh produce quickly before it loses flavor. Always use kosher or other additive-free salt; iodized table salt will turn some pickles a dark color.

Citron Pickle

Fragrant Meyer lemons and aromatic yuzu citrons are two of the delights of early winter. Meyer lemon is rounder, smoother, and less acidic than more common varieties. Ask for it in your produce department. Yuzu citrons can be found in Japanese markets from November through January.

4 to 6 servings

2 YUZU CITRONS OR MEYER LEMONS
8 TABLESPOONS SUGAR
1 CUP SAKE
PINCH OF SALT

Rough up the citron's skin all over with a grater. Cut it into quarters, place it in a nonreactive pot, and cover it with cold water. Bring it just to a boil, reduce the heat, and simmer for 5 minutes. Drain the citron, cover it with cold water, and let it soak for at least 5 hours to remove bitterness.

Combine the citron, 5 tablespoons of the sugar, the sake, and salt in the nonreactive pot. Simmer for 30 minutes. Transfer the citron and cooking liquid to a heat-resistant glass container. When cool, cover and refrigerate it overnight.

About 2 hours before serving, cut away and discard the fruit and white pith. Place the peel on a cutting board, skin side down, and use a small, sharp knife to scrape away any remaining pith, leaving the paper-thin skin. Sprinkle the skin with the remaining 3 tablespoons sugar, cover, and set aside.

Just before serving, rinse the pickled citron. Drain it on paper towels, and cut it into 1¼-inch triangles. Arrange two triangles with other foods on each tray or plate.

Pickled Okra

Look for fresh okra in the fall. It's wonderful simmered in soups, served lightly steamed on a tray with other foods, or pickled to give your menu a Southern flavor. The pepper and mustard make these pickles hot. Combine them with a sweeter variety, like the chrysanthemum pickles, for balance.

3 pints

1 POUND FRESH OKRA
½ SMALL, DRIED, RED CHILI PEPPER
2¼ CUPS RICE VINEGAR
3 TABLESPOONS KOSHER SALT
1½ CUPS WATER
1½ TEASPOONS YELLOW MUSTARD SEEDS

Sterilize 3 (1-pint) canning jars and 3 sets of lids and rings in boiling water.

Wash the okra and trim the stems, but don't remove the caps.

Seed the chili pepper, and cut it into 6 pieces.

Put a large canning pot of water on to boil.

Bring the vinegar, salt, and water to a boil in a nonreactive pot, and remove it from the heat.

Evenly divide the chili pepper and mustard seeds among the sterilized jars. Add the okra, alternating the direction of the caps.

Pour the hot vinegar liquid into the jars, leaving ½ inch of space beneath the rim. Wipe the rims with a damp cloth. Place the lids and rings on the jars, and turn the screw band firmly without forcing.

Use long-handled tongs or a wire jar holder to submerge the jars in the boiling water bath, making sure they don't touch. Simmer for 15 minutes.

Remove the jars with the tongs or jar holder, and let them cool for 24 hours. Let the pickles mellow in a cool place for 6 to 8 weeks before using.

Before serving, remove the okra caps with a diagonal cut, and discard them. Cut each pickle into 2 diagonal pieces. Mound them in a bowl with the cut side facing the guests. Store opened jars of pickles in the refrigerator.

Pickled Watermelon Rind

New varieties of watermelon seem to appear in the markets each summer. One year, I experimented with yellow watermelon for these pickles. Their pale, translucent color looked beautiful paired with green pickled cucumbers and pink ginger shoots. A 9- or 10-pound watermelon will yield about 2 pounds of rind.

2 pints

2 POUNDS WATERMELON RIND

2 TABLESPOONS KOSHER SALT

4 INCHES FRESH GINGER

2 CUPS RICE VINEGAR

1 CUP SUGAR

1 CUP WATER

Scrape the rind with a spoon to remove any bits of flesh. Peel away the green skin with a small, sharp knife or vegetable peeler, and discard it. Cut the rind lengthwise into 1-inch strips, and cut the strips into 2-inch pieces.

Place the rind in a bowl, sprinkle it with the salt, and cover it with cold water. Refrigerate it overnight.

Rinse the rind two or three times in cold water, and drain well.

Peel the ginger, and cut it into ¼-inch slices.

Put the ginger in a large, nonreactive pot with the vinegar, sugar, and 1 cup water. Heat it, stirring, until the sugar dissolves. Add the rind, bring it to a simmer, and cook it, partially covered, for about 45 minutes, until tender.

Sterilize 2 (1-pint) canning jars and 2 sets of lids and rings in boiling water.

Put a large canning pot of water on to boil.

Pack the rind in the hot jars. Ladle in the hot syrup to within ½ inch of the rim. Wipe the rims with a damp cloth. Put on the lids and rings, and turn the screw band firmly without forcing.

Use long-handled tongs or a wire jar holder to submerge the jars in the boiling water bath, making sure they don't touch. Simmer for 30 minutes.

Remove the jars with the tongs or jar holder, and let them cool. Store them in a cool place for 2 to 3 weeks so the pickles can mellow. Refrigerate opened jars.

Quick Cucumber-Shiso Pickles

The delight of this pickle is the unusual flavor of shiso, a culinary herb with hints of cinnamon and mint.

4 to 6 servings

> 4 SMALL JAPANESE CUCUMBERS (ABOUT 1 POUND)
> 1 TEASPOON SEA SALT
> 1½ TABLESPOONS MINCED SHISO LEAVES
> DASH OF CAYENNE
> 1½ TEASPOONS SUGAR
> 1½ TABLESPOONS RICE VINEGAR

Cut the unpeeled cucumbers into thin slices. Toss them with the salt and 1 tablespoon of the shiso leaves. Set them aside in a colander for 30 to 60 minutes, tossing and squeezing occasionally to extract the liquid. When the cucumbers have given up most of their liquid, rinse them well under cold water, and gently squeeze them dry.

Stir together the remaining shiso, cayenne, sugar, and rice vinegar until the sugar dissolves. Pour the mixture onto the cucumbers and toss them well. Serve immediately or cover and chill. The pickles keep for 2 days in the refrigerator.

Vinegared Cucumbers

These crunchy pickles are refreshing in summer.

4 to 6 servings

> 4 SMALL JAPANESE CUCUMBERS (ABOUT 1 POUND)
> ½ TEASPOON SEA SALT
> 1 PIECE KOMBU SEAWEED, 3 BY 3 INCHES
> 3 TABLESPOONS RICE VINEGAR
> 1 TABLESPOON SUGAR
> 2 OR 3 DROPS OF SOY SAUCE

Peel thin strips of skin from the cucumbers, leaving a few strips of green, and cut them into ½-inch diagonal slices. Sprinkle the slices with the salt, and let them sit in a colander for 5 minutes. Rinse the cucumber, and gently squeeze it dry.

Cut the kombu into fine shreds with scissors; you should have about ⅛ cup. Toss the kombu with the cucumber in a glass bowl.

Stir together the vinegar, sugar, and soy sauce until the sugar dissolves. Pour over the cucumber mixture.

Place the mixture in a pickle press if you have one. If not, mound the mixture on a large plate, place another plate on top, and weight it with rocks or cans of beans. Let the pickles sit for 2 to 3 hours.

Drain the pickles well, and serve at room temperature within a few hours. Leftovers don't keep well.

Cucumber-Mirin Salsa

This bright, tart East-West combination is a fine accompaniment to Tempura Chicken with Asparagus *(page 106)* or grilled fish. Use only the best-quality rice vinegar.

4 servings

2 SMALL JAPANESE CUCUMBERS (ABOUT ½ POUND)

¼ SMALL RED ONION

½ RED BELL PEPPER

1 TABLESPOON CHOPPED FRESH SHISO OR MINT LEAVES

¼ CUP RICE VINEGAR

2 TABLESPOONS MIRIN

SEA SALT

Peel and dice the cucumbers and onion. Seed and dice the red pepper. Stir the vegetables and shiso together in a glass dish. Add the vinegar, mirin, and salt to taste. Cover and chill for an hour before serving.

Chrysanthemum Daikon Pickle

Fashioned in the shape of chrysanthemum blossoms with yellow flecks of lemon in the center, these crisp pickles are a wonderful accompaniment or garnish to almost any meal.

4 to 6 servings

> ½ CUP RICE VINEGAR
> 2½ TABLESPOONS SUGAR
> ½ CUP WATER
> 1 MEDIUM DAIKON
> 1 LEMON

Combine the vinegar, sugar, and water in a small, nonreactive saucepan. Bring just to a boil, stirring to dissolve the sugar. Set it aside to cool.

Cut off and discard the thick daikon peel (rabbits love to eat them). Slice the daikon into 1-inch-thick rounds. Cut each round into quarters, and trim the quarters to form squares.

To make the chrysanthemum petals, place 2 chopsticks on opposite sides of a radish square. Hold a long, sharp knife perpendicular to the chopsticks, and make 4 or 5 evenly spaced cuts across the square; the chopsticks will prevent the knife from cutting all the way through. Turn the daikon square and repeat so that you have a grid pattern. Score all the daikon slices in the same way.

Cover the daikon with the sweetened vinegar, and marinate for 20 minutes. Meanwhile, slice thin chips of yellow peel from the lemon.

To serve, drain the daikon, and spread the "petals" of the slices. Place a chip of lemon peel in the center of each one.

Pickled Ginger Flower

Myoga is the name of the flower bud in a particular species of ginger plant in season in late summer. It's exotic even for the Japanese. Look for it in specialty produce markets. Cut into quarters, these pickled buds reveal the delicate ginger petals ready to open.

6 to 8 servings

1 POUND MYOGA
1 CUP RICE VINEGAR
⅓ CUP SUGAR
1 TABLESPOON SEA SALT

Peel off the outer leaves of the buds.

Stir together the vinegar, sugar, and salt until dissolved.

Place the myoga in a shallow glass dish, and pour on the vinegar mixture. Cover and marinate overnight at room temperature.

Drain the buds, and cut them lengthwise into quarters. Keep the slices together in pairs. Taste one; if it's too tart, rinse and drain it before serving.

Green Plum Pickles

In May, you'll find baskets of tiny green plums, ready for pickling, in Japanese markets. Green, unripe apricots may be substituted. Reminiscent of brandied fruit, these pickles keep indefinitely.

6 to 8 servings

1 POUND HARD GREEN JAPANESE PLUMS
8 TEASPOONS SEA SALT
1 CUP SUGAR
1 CUP VODKA

Prick each plum 2 or 3 times with a needle. Cover them with water, and let them soak for 24 hours.

Drain the plums, and sprinkle them with the salt while still wet. Mix well, cover, and let stand at room temperature for 3 days.

Rinse the plums well, and remove the pits by squeezing the fruit or cutting it open. Cover the pitted plums with water, and let them soak at room temperature for 12 hours to eliminate any salt.

Drain the plums, and transfer them to a jar with a tight lid. Stir the sugar into the vodka until it dissolves. Pour the sweetened vodka over the plums, cover the jar tightly, and keep it in a cool place for at least 2 months before using.

Pickled Ginger

If you've eaten sushi, you're probably familiar with the pale pink pickled ginger typically served with it. Pickled ginger is readily available in Oriental markets and large grocery stores, but it's usually made with lots of chemical preservatives. Try making your own for an incomparably fresh taste.

4 to 6 servings

½ POUND FRESH GINGERROOT

SEA SALT

1 CUP RICE VINEGAR

7 TABLESPOONS WATER

3 ½ TABLESPOONS SUGAR

Peel the ginger, put it in a shallow bowl, and sprinkle it lightly with salt. Let sit overnight at room temperature.

Stir together the vinegar, water, and sugar until the sugar dissolves.

Rinse and drain the ginger, and put it in a glass container. Pour on the marinade, cover the container, and refrigerate it for 7 days. The ginger will turn slightly pink.

Cut the pickled ginger with the grain into paper-thin slices. Serve it in a small mound next to sushi.

Pickled Ginger Shoots

Look for ginger shoots in the spring in Oriental markets.

1 pint

    ½ POUND FRESH GINGER SHOOTS
    1 CUP RICE VINEGAR
    7 TABLESPOONS WATER
    3½ TABLESPOONS SUGAR

Bring a large pot of water to a boil.

Have a clean, 1-pint canning jar ready.

Separate the shoots and clean them. Plunge them into the boiling water, and immediately drain them to prevent limpness.

Heat the vinegar, water, and sugar in a small, nonreactive pan until the sugar dissolves.

Pack the ginger shoots on end in the canning jar, and cover them with the hot marinade. The shoots will turn pinkish and be ready to use in 3 or 4 hours. Store the pickled shoots, covered, in the refrigerator; they will keep indefinitely, and you can add more shoots to the marinade as you use the pickled ones.

Recipes

Sweets and Fruits

The focal point of any tea gathering is the preparation of tea. The tea bowl is rinsed with hot water and wiped dry in circular motions with a dampened white linen cloth. The powdered green tea is scooped in. Hot water is poured into the bowl and a small bamboo whisk with featherlight tines whips the tea into a froth.

The guests take one sip, then another. The taste is delicate, yet slightly bitter. Sweets served just moments before balance and heighten the flavor. The guests ask the name of the tea and where it was blended, and remark on the taste and preparation of the sweets. They ask if the sweets have a poetic name.

Okashi, or sweet making, is a highly respected art. Many famous shops in Japan specialize in the sweets for Chanoyu; in San Francisco, Yamada Seika carries on the tradition. I often visit Mr. Yamada at his store to buy sweets for tea. He is always busy in front of a mountain of red bean paste, working quickly to form the small bean sweets that will be folded into cherry leaves in April or covered with a red-and-yellow pastry to resemble mountains in autumn. His sweets are a pleasure to eat, their flavor and texture always delectable.

During a formal tea gathering, two kinds of tea and two kinds of sweets are served. Following the Kaiseki meal, moist, trufflelike sweets are served in stacked lacquer boxes, one for each guest. A single bowl of thick tea, Koicha, is made for the guests to share. Each person takes two or three sips, wipes where he has drunk with a tiny linen cloth, and passes the tea bowl to the next guest. The Koicha, thick and rich like pesto sauce, is blended from the finest leaves of the tea plant.

A second sweet is served to accompany the thin, cappuccino-like tea that follows. The pressed sugars are a marvel of color, shape, and design. Two or three kinds are arranged on a tray: miniature seashells and butterflies in spring, white waterfalls paired with green maple leaves in early summer. In autumn, tiny pine needles, red maple leaves, acorns, and chrysanthemum flowers are arranged in a basket as though blown together by a cool breeze. The variety is endless and never fails to enchant the guests. In the same spirit, you can serve pressed watermelon and lemon drops in summer, or Vermont maple sugar leaves or Boston baked bean candies in autumn. Better yet, make your own trufflelike sweets and give them poetic names. Use the Basic Sweet Bean Paste recipe that follows, subtly coloring and shaping it according to the season.

Basic Sweet Bean Paste

Most trufflelike sweets are made from a sweetened bean paste called "an." The paste can be made in advance and kept wrapped for 2 to 3 days in the refrigerator or frozen for up to 6 months. Cannellini beans make a pure white an that can be colored in wonderful shades of pale pink, purple, yellow, lavender, and so forth. Use a commercial food coloring, and add only a drop or two at a time until the color is just right.

About 25 sweets

1 POUND DRIED CANNELLINI BEANS
¾ CUP SUGAR
1½ TABLESPOONS CORN SYRUP

Sort through the beans, and discard any stones. Soak the beans overnight in abundant water; the beans will expand.

Drain the soaked beans, and put them into a large pot with water to cover. Bring them to a boil, occasionally skimming the foam with a fine-mesh strainer. After about 45 minutes, the skins will begin slipping from the beans. Drain them, cover with fresh water, and bring them back to a boil. Add ½ cup cold water to the pot, reduce the heat, and simmer until soft, about 45 minutes, occasionally skimming the foam. Add more water if needed, so the beans are always covered.

Drain the cooked beans, put them in a large bowl, and cover them with cold water. Gently stir them with a fine-mesh strainer, skimming off any foam. Drain and rinse the beans two or three more times, until the water stays clear.

Puree the beans in a food processor. Add enough water to make a thin liquid. Pour the bean liquid through a fine sieve or strainer into a large bowl. Use a rubber spatula to press the beans through the sieve. Add more water, a little at a time, and continue to press until only the skins and bean pulp remain. Discard them. Place the strained liquid in a cloth bag, and squeeze out as much water as possible.

Transfer the bean paste to a large, heavy-bottomed pot, and stir in the sugar; the bean paste will liquefy. Cook it over low heat, stirring constantly, for about 30 minutes, until the paste becomes thicker than mashed potatoes. Add the corn syrup and cook for 5 minutes more, taking care that the paste doesn't burn.

Place a damp cloth over a cutting board, and turn the paste onto it to cool. Wrap it in plastic wrap, and refrigerate it until needed.

Chrysanthemum Flower Sweets

Serve these sweets with whisked bowls of green tea in the fall, and share stories with your guests about the magical chrysanthemum flower and its powers of eternal youth.

About 25 sweets

 1 LARGE SWEET POTATO
 4 CUPS WATER
 1 RECIPE BASIC SWEET BEAN PASTE *(page 173)*

Peel the sweet potato, cut it into rounds, and immediately place it in a pot with the water. Cook over medium heat until soft, about 20 minutes. Drain the sweet potato, and push it through a fine sieve two or three times until finely mashed. Mix in 2 tablespoons of the Basic Sweet Bean Paste to make the sweet potato firmer.

Roll the sweet potato mixture into balls the size of walnuts. You should have about 25.

Shape the remaining Basic Sweet Bean Paste into an equal number of disks about 3 inches across and ¼ inch thick.

Place a sweet potato ball in the center of each bean paste disk. Press and mold the disk about ¾ of the way up the ball, leaving a little bit of yellow sweet potato peeking out at the top.

Dampen and squeeze out a small tea towel, and lay it open in one hand. Place the assembled bean paste in the center of the towel. Gently wrap the towel around the paste, twisting the top of the towel to form a rounded shape in your hand. Unwrap the towel. The finished sweet should have a round shape, and a pattern left by the cloth. The yellow sweet potato should peek out from the top. Repeat with the remaining bean paste.

Serve on small plates. The sweets can be refrigerated for up to a day.

Japanese Truffles

The poetic name for this elegant lavender, white, and pale yellow sweet is Chinese Robes. It's traditionally served in May, just before the irises bloom, and it looks stunning on black lacquer plates.

About 14 sweets

> 1 RECIPE BASIC SWEET BEAN PASTE *(page 173)*, modified as
>   directed below
> PURPLE FOOD COLORING
> 1 RAW EGG YOLK
> 2 HARD-BOILED EGG YOLKS, PRESSED THROUGH A SIEVE

When making the sweet bean paste, divide it into thirds before adding the sugar. Place two thirds of the paste in a heavy pan, and mix in ½ cup sugar. Cook over low heat, stirring constantly, for about 30 minutes, until the paste becomes thicker than mashed potatoes. Stir in 1 tablespoon of the corn syrup, and cook 5 minutes more. Turn it out onto a damp cloth to cool. Divide it in two. Leave one half white, and color the other half with the food coloring, kneading in a drop at a time until it's a pale purple. Set aside.

Cook the remaining bean paste as above with the remaining ¼ cup sugar. When thick, stir in the remaining ½ tablespoon corn syrup. Put about ½ cup of the bean paste mixture into a small bowl, and quickly stir in the raw egg yolk. Return the mixture to the pot, and cook over low heat for 5 more minutes, stirring continually. Remove it from the heat, and stir in the sieved egg yolks. Turn the yellow paste out onto a damp cloth to cool.

To assemble, roll the yellow paste into balls the size of walnuts; you will have about 14.

Shape the white bean paste into an equal number of disks about 3 inches wide and ¼ inch thick.

Place a yellow ball in the center of a white disk. Press and mold the disk about ¾ of the way up the ball, leaving a little bit of yellow peeking out at the top. Place about 1 teaspoon of the purple paste on the top to cover the yellow center. It should look like a little hat.

Dampen and squeeze out a tea towel, and lay it open in one hand. Place the assembled bean paste in the center of the towel. Gently wrap the towel around the paste, twisting the top to form a rounded shape in your hand. Unwrap the towel. The finished sweet should have a round shape, and a pattern left by the cloth. The purple paste should merge with the white, leaving a design of purple and white with the yellow filling inside. Repeat with the remaining dough.

Serve on small black lacquer dishes if you have them. The sweets will keep in the refrigerator for up to a day.

Snow on Brushwood

This trufflelike sweet is made with two kinds of sweetened bean paste, one from dark red *azuki* beans, the other from white cannellini beans. The white paste is passed through a large sieve, creating curls that are placed on the dark red paste to look like newly fallen snow on a pile of brushwood. If you have frozen bean paste on hand, it will make preparation much easier.

About 25 sweets

1 RECIPE BASIC SWEET BEAN PASTE *(page 173)*
1 POUND AZUKI BEANS
¾ CUP SUGAR
1½ TABLESPOONS CORN SYRUP

Use the azuki beans, sugar, and corn syrup to make the red bean paste as directed in the Basic Sweet Bean Paste recipe.

To assemble, roll the red bean paste into balls about ¾ inch in diameter; you should have about 25. Set them aside on a plate.

Press the white paste through a wide-mesh sieve (with ⅛-inch openings) to form curly shapes. Use chopsticks or tweezers to place the curls one by one on the tops and sides of the red bean paste balls. Cover thickly to look like snow that has fallen on brushwood.

Serve on individual plates. The sweets will keep in the refrigerator for up to a day.

Zenzai (Sweet Bean Soup)

Zenzai is traditionally served in November to celebrate the annual change in the tea room when the brazier is removed and the sunken hearth is opened. This celebration, called Robiraki (Ro is the sunken hearth), is considered the tea person's New Year. The first large fire of the year welcomes the dark evenings and chill air of autumn. This hot, sweet broth with mochi delights the guests before drinking tea. The beans should be salty, the broth clear.

4 to 6 servings

2 CUPS AZUKI BEANS
½ CUP SUGAR
3 ½ TEASPOONS USUKUCHI (LIGHT) SOY SAUCE
PINCH OF SALT
4 MOCHI CAKES, CUT INTO QUARTERS

Pick through the beans and discard any stones. Rinse them with cold water.

Place the beans in a large, heavy-bottomed pot with 1 cup water. Cover the pot and bring the beans to a boil. Add another cup of cold water, cover, and return to a boil. Add 4 more cups of cold water, reduce the heat, and simmer the beans, partially covered, for about 40 minutes, adding extra water if needed so the beans are always covered. The beans are done when they are soft but not losing their skins, firm but not mushy.

Drain the beans, put them into a large bowl of cold water, and stir them gently. Drain and repeat two or three times, until the water remains clear.

In a large, heavy-bottomed saucepan, cook the sugar and ½ cup water over medium heat. When the sugar water comes to a boil, add the beans. Simmer for 15 minutes, adding more water if needed to cover the beans.

Remove the saucepan from the heat, and season the beans with the soy sauce and salt. Cool, cover, and refrigerate overnight.

Up to 4 hours before serving, broil the mochi as directed on *page 49*. You will have leftovers; mochi easily becomes overcrisp, and it's good to make extra. Choose pieces that are perfectly golden brown for the soup.

To serve, reheat the soup, making sure it's piping hot. Place 2 pieces of mochi per person in the pot with the soup. Cover the mochi with bean liquid and let it warm and soften for 2 or 3 minutes. For each serving, ladle a portion of soup into a deep soup bowl. Top it with 2 pieces of mochi, and ladle on a little more soup so the mochi peeks out from under the beans. Serve immediately.

Persimmon with Meyer Lemon

I had never tasted persimmons until I moved to California, where I noticed them everywhere in the markets during the fall. Now I make persimmon pudding for Thanksgiving, toss them in a spinach salad with sesame dressing, and serve them plain for dessert with a sprinkling of sweet Meyer lemon. Choose firm persimmons for this dish.

4 to 6 servings

4 Fuyu persimmons
1 Meyer lemon

Peel and seed the persimmons, and cut them into ¼-inch slices. Just before serving, cut the lemon in half, and squeeze a little juice on the persimmons.

Sweetened Kumquats

Kumquats are a festive New Year's food, arranged in stacked black lacquer boxes.

4 servings

1 POUND KUMQUATS, STEMS REMOVED
1 CUP SUGAR
4 CUPS WATER

Prick each kumquat a couple of times with a skewer, to keep them from shriveling when cooked. Put them in a saucepan, cover them with water, and simmer for 10 minutes to remove any bitterness. Drain and remove.

Heat the sugar and 4 cups water in the same pan until the sugar has dissolved. Add the kumquats, and gently simmer partially covered for 30 minutes. Remove from the heat. Place in a glass container with the cooking liquid and refrigerate, covered, overnight.

Drain the marinade, and save it for making another batch. Serve the kumquats at room temperature.

Muscat Grapes with Mustard Dressing

The mustard picks up the mysterious fragrance and taste of the muscat grapes. This dish is a perfect Indian summer appetizer or autumn dessert. It takes time and patience to peel and seed the grapes, but it's well worth the effort.

4 servings

1 POUND MUSCAT GRAPES
1 TABLESPOON DRY MUSTARD
1 TEASPOON WATER
1 TABLESPOON WHITE MISO
4 TABLESPOONS UNSEASONED DASHI *(page 53)*
½ TEASPOON SOY SAUCE

Peel, halve, and seed the grapes. Set them aside.

Mix the mustard and water to form a paste. Blend in the miso, and slowly add the dashi, stirring until the ingredients have dissolved. Season with the soy sauce.

Just before serving, gently toss the grapes with the dressing.

Mission Figs with Miso Topping

Serve this quick, beautiful dish in the fall when freshly harvested figs are abundant.

4 servings

> 4 TABLESPOONS WHITE MISO
>
> 1 ½ TABLESPOONS SAKE
>
> 1 TEASPOON SUGAR
>
> 1 TABLESPOON FRESH GINGER JUICE *(page 49)*
>
> 6 LARGE RIPE MISSION FIGS, HALVED LENGTHWISE

Heat the broiler. Line a baking sheet with foil.

In a small saucepan, heat the miso, sake, sugar, and ginger juice over low heat for about a minute, until the sauce becomes shiny.

Place the figs, cut side up, on the prepared baking sheet, and broil them as close to the heat as possible until they brown on the edges, about 2 minutes.

Spoon a little sauce on each fig, and serve.

Kiwi with Chrysanthemum Petals

Make this dish in late August when chrysanthemums are in bloom. Only petals from yellow chrysanthemums are edible. They look beautiful tossed with cool, green kiwis.

4 to 6 servings

    10 FRESHLY PICKED YELLOW CHRYSANTHEMUM FLOWERS
    6 TABLESPOONS RICE VINEGAR
    2 TABLESPOONS SUGAR
    1 TEASPOON SALT
    4 RIPE KIWIS

Pluck the outer petals from the flowers. (The tightly closed inner petals are too bitter to use.) Bring a pot of water to a boil, and plunge in the petals for just a second. Drain them immediately, and rinse under cold water.

Stir the vinegar, sugar, and salt together in a mixing bowl until dissolved. Add the petals and toss. Let them sit for 5 minutes. Drain and gently squeeze dry.

Peel the kiwis and cut them into thin slices. Toss them with the chrysanthemum petals, and serve mounded on a tray or in individual dishes.

Blueberry Brocade Jewel

In this summer recipe, the crystal-clear sweet is layered with a "brocade" of fresh blueberries. Kanten, which is made of seaweed, acts just like gelatin and is much better for you. Don't be dismayed by the amount of sugar in this recipe; it just highlights the fresh, tart flavor of the blueberries.

6 to 8 servings

1 QUART FRESH BLUEBERRIES
4 STICKS KANTEN (1 PACKAGE OF 14 GRAMS)
1¼ CUPS WATER
2 CUPS SUGAR

Wash and stem the blueberries, discarding any bruised ones. Set them aside in a colander to drain.

Soak the kanten in water to cover for an hour. Drain and squeeze dry.

Dampen an 8-inch square baking pan with a removable insert. If you don't have one, line an 8-inch square pan with foil, letting the foil extend over two ends.

Tear the kanten into pieces, and put it into a heavy-bottomed pot with the water. Bring it to a simmer and cook, stirring constantly, until the kanten has dissolved, about 10 minutes.

Remove the pot from the heat, strain the liquid through a fine sieve, and return it to the pot. Add the sugar and bring it to a boil, stirring constantly. Cook until it reaches 120° F. on a candy thermometer.

Pour the kanten into the prepared baking pan. Skim off any bubbles with a folded piece of paper. Let it set for 5 to 10 minutes.

Drop the berries onto the kanten until the surface is completely covered. You want them to sink as much as possible. Refrigerate for an hour or two, until completely set.

To serve, run a knife around the edges of the pan, and lift out the insert or foil. Cut the kanten into 1½-inch squares. Serve in small stacked black lacquer boxes or on individual dishes.

Variation:

Cook the kanten liquid as directed, and tint it a pale blue with food coloring. Pour it into tiny, individual sweets molds, and drop a ripe raspberry in the center of each one. Chill to set, and unmold to serve.

Glossary

Tea Terms

Chaji: A formal tea gathering. There are seven types, including Asa Chaji, held in the early morning hours of summer; Yobanashi Chaji, or "night-speaking tea," held on winter evenings; and Hango Chaji, an abbreviated midday tea that can be held in any season.

Chanoyu: The Way of Tea. It encompasses the tea ceremony and the connoisseurship of the fine and applied arts, as well as the study of literature, flower arranging, garden design, architecture, and Kaiseki cuisine that are associated with it.

Hashiarai: The fourth course of the Kaiseki meal, consisting of seasoned hot water to refresh the palate.

Hassun: The fifth and most poetic course of the Kaiseki meal, consisting of two foods, one loosely categorized as from the "mountain" and the other from the "sea," served on a plain cedar tray.

Kaiseki: The light, simple, elegant cuisine associated with Chanoyu. Long considered Japan's haute cuisine, it emphasizes beautiful presentation and the use of fresh, seasonal ingredients.

Koicha: A thick tea with a pesto-like consistency served at formal tea gatherings.

Matcha: The finely ground green tea served at tea gatherings. It is whisked into a thick froth with hot water, producing a sort of Japanese cappuccino.

Nimono: The second course of the Kaiseki meal, consisting of a seasoned broth with seasonal ingredients. It is considered the heart of the meal.

Tenshin Chakai: A less formal Kaiseki meal, consisting of a soup, tidbits of food served on a tray, sake, sweets, and tea.

Wabi: A plain, unpolished beauty. It was at the heart of the aesthetic created by early Japanese tea masters.

Yakimono: The third course of the Kaiseki meal, consisting of a grilled food that is always served alone.

Ingredients

Azuki beans: These sweet and flavorful small dry red beans are grown in Japan and the United States. They are quick to cook and the easiest of all beans to digest. In Kaiseki cooking, they are often used for making an, the bean paste used in sweets.

Broccoli rabe: The flower shoot of a kind of turnip with a tantalizing sharp but sweet flavor. It looks like a leafy broccoli with tiny broccoli-like florets.

Cilantro: Also known as fresh coriander and Chinese parsley, this herb is widely used in Asian and Mexican cooking. It looks like a flat-leaf parsley, but has a strong and pungent flavor.

Cucumber: The Japanese cucumber is seedless, and is less watery and thinner skinned than common varieties.

Daikon: This large white radish is available most of the year, but is most abundant in fall and winter. Its snow-white appearance is lovely against black lacquer or deep-colored plates. High in vitamin C and enzymes that aid in digestion, it is prized for its healthful properties and is usually served grated with tempura to help digest cooking oil. Takuan, or daikon pickle, is served for the full-course Kaiseki meal; look for it in Japanese markets. The pickling process turns the radish a bright yellow.

Eggplant: The Japanese eggplant is a small and elongated variety of the large, dark purple globe used in most Mediterranean cooking. It is also sweeter, has a thinner skin, and is less watery.

Ginger: Use fresh gingerroot for its wonderful tangy flavor. It is often made into a pale pink, thinly sliced pickle called gari, usually served with sushi and sashimi. Keep it refrigerated. Ground ginger is not a substitute.

Jicama: This crisp, sweet, and refreshing Mexican root vegetable is brown on the outside and pure white on the inside.

Kanten or agar-agar: A seaweed that acts exactly like gelatin and is much healthier for you. It comes in powder, flakes, or bars and can be found in Japanese markets and natural food stores. The bars are more commonly found in Japanese markets, and are the easiest to use.

Katsuo (bonito flakes): Bonito is a dried fish that is shaved into flakes. It deepens and enriches the dashi used for flavoring many of the recipes. Always check the label to make sure the fish is bonito and not dried mackerel. My favorite brand, Well-Pac Hanakatsuo, comes in a box with a colorful design of a fish in waves.

Kombu: A wide, thick, dark green seaweed. The giant kelp is dried in the sun, cut, folded, and packaged. Many of the recipes in this book depend on its subtle flavoring. Look for dried kelp that is 3 or 4 inches wide and up to 12 inches long and folded over. Always buy the best quality, and never wash or rinse it. Like other sea vegetables, it is rich in nutrients. It has recently been discovered that kombu broth lowers blood pressure and improves the condition of the heart.

Lemongrass: An aromatic grass with a rich lemon flavor used in Southeast Asian and tropical cooking. You can buy it dried, in stores that sell herbs and spices, or you can buy it fresh from your local grocer. A small sliver of fresh lemongrass is used in Kaiseki cooking as the fragrance placed on top of soup ingredients. It's not edible, but releases a wonderful flavor and scent.

Lotus root: A root vegetable with white, crunchy flesh that grows in links like a sausage's. Tubular hollows run the length of each link, and make a beautiful pattern when sliced crosswise. Fresh lotus root, in season in late fall and winter, is available in Oriental markets. Choose firm, unblemished roots. Once peeled, the flesh will discolor almost immediately, so always immerse it in lightly vinegared water.

Meyer lemons: Sweeter than regular lemons, they have a smooth skin and a deep yellow color. Their wonderful tangy flavor and aroma are perfect for the fragrance and zest in soups and salads.

Mirin: This sweet rice wine is a staple of Japanese cooking.

Miso: A paste made from fermented soybeans and sea salt that is used to make creamy soups and sauces. It's rich in protein and comes in different flavors, strengths, and brands. The three basic types are sweet, medium salty, and salty. Generally, the lighter the color, the sweeter the miso. White and yellow Saikyo miso are sweet. Red miso is salty with a strong flavor. The medium to golden colored shiro miso is milder than the red, but still salty and strong. Buy the brand with the fewest additives and preservatives. Keep miso unopened in the freezer indefinitely. After opening, reseal and keep in the freezer for up to 6 months.

Mitsuba: Also known as trefoil, this member of the parsley family has a flavor between sorrel and celery. Wild chervil is a good substitute. Always look for bunches that are fresh, with young green leaves. Wrapped in plastic, it keeps in the refrigerator for a week.

Mizuna greens: This pot herb mustard is becoming more popular in the United States. The sweet, tangy flavor of the dark green leaves is wonderful in salads and soups.

Mochi: Chewy cakes made from pounded, hot, glutinous rice. Buy fresh ones if you can find them in Japanese markets. They are also available frozen. When cooked under the broiler, they puff up and brown. Mochi are a wonderful ingredient in the sweet bean soup called zenzai.

Muscat grapes: Grown in the mountains and valleys of wine country, these aromatic grapes are in season for a short time in autumn.

Mushrooms: The Japanese use shiitake mushrooms in all their cooking. While fresh shiitakes are now available in American supermarkets, dried ones are better for Kaiseki cooking. Their flavor is more condensed. Look for packages of 8 to 10 medium-small dried shiitakes, with cracks in the thick rounded caps. They keep indefinitely. Always discard the stems, or save them for soup stock. Fresh shiitakes and other wild mushrooms, like chanterelles, are wonderful to grill or simmer for soups. Chanterelles are in season in the fall and winter; shiitakes are commercially grown and are available year-round.

Noodles: One of Japan's most popular foods. Soba noodles are made from buckwheat flour and have a nutty, toasted flavor. Somen noodles are thin, white wheat noodles that are often eaten cold in summer.

Nori: A sea vegetable that is dried into thin square sheets measuring 7 by 8 inches. Nori is roasted over a flame until it becomes green-gold and looks like exotic handmade paper. It is used to make sushi and can also be cut into strips for tasty condiments and garnishes.

Persimmons: Hachiya persimmons have a pointed shape, and need to ripen at room temperature until soft. Fuyu persimmons are a larger, round variety that can be eaten when still firm. Peel the skin of the fruit before eating. It's considered good luck to leave a few persimmons hanging from the tree in autumn after all the leaves have fallen.

Pumpkins: Kabocha and Hokkaido are small, sweet-tasting pumpkins in season in the autumn and early winter. They have yellow flesh and green skin.

Rice vinegar: A light, slightly sweet vinegar made from naturally fermented rice. It's milder than Western vinegars.

Sake: This rice wine is an important ingredient in Kaiseki cooking. It's used in many recipes and is a main flavoring ingredient for soup stock. It's widely distributed in America. There are three grades of sake: special class, first class, and second class. The special class, ikkyu, should be used for Kaiseki. One of the best brands to serve your guests during the Kaiseki meal is Genbei San no Oni Koroshi. It comes in a large bottle with a delightful picture of a devil on the label. Sake is served hot, but make sure you never boil it. Heat it in a small glass pot set in a double boiler. For Kaiseki, serve it from a small iron kettle with a patterned porcelain lid. Sake cups are very small, just enough for a few sips. The pleasure is in the pouring.

Sansho: The leaves of the prickly ash plant have a delicate and aromatic flavor. The leaf is used as a garnish or seasoning. It's hard to find fresh sansho leaves in markets, but you can grow sansho in your kitchen garden. It also comes in a dried powder, called sansho pepper.

Sesame seeds: Roasted, ground, and seasoned sesame seeds are used often in Kaiseki sauces. They are usually roasted on the stove top, and the aroma is one of the pleasures of Kaiseki cooking. Buy white sesame seeds that are not hulled. Black sesame seeds are used as garnish.

Shiso: Also known as perilla or beefsteak plant, this member of the mint family has the aroma of cinnamon in its maturing flower and of cumin in its fresh leaves. The large, spade-shaped leaf may be purple or green. Shiso is native to India and China, and is used in Burmese, Indian, Chinese, and Japanese cuisines. Asian food markets and some supermarkets carry it. It can also be grown from seed. To store shiso, wrap it in a dampened paper towel, place it in a plastic bag, and refrigerate.

Soy sauce: This rich-tasting, fermented soybean product is also called shoyu. I use it instead of salt to deepen the flavors of my cooking. There are many brands and types of soy sauce, and each has a different flavor and strength. Usukuchi soy sauce is lighter in color than regular soy sauce, but it's much saltier. It's used to avoid darkening the color of clear broth soups and other dishes. Use it sparingly.

Tamari: A thick soy sauce often served in restaurants with sashimi. For most of the recipes in this book, I use San-J Reduced Sodium Tamari Soy Sauce. I buy it at a natural foods store, and it tastes as good as one of the most expensive brands, Maruman Tezukuri Shoyu, in my Japanese market. Neither brand contains additives or preservatives. Try different brands to find the one you like the best.

Tofu: This staple of vegetarian and Asian cooking is made from soybeans. The beans are cooked, then blended with water and mixed with a natural solidifier. The resulting curds are pressed into small cakes that come in firm, regular, and soft varieties. Freshly made tofu is delicious with a little soy sauce and ginger. I prefer tofu made with no additives; experiment with brands to see which you like the best. Tofu is high in protein, and has been shown to lower cholesterol levels.

Umeboshi: These pickled plums are found in every Japanese household. In June, when green plums are in season, they are soaked in brine and packed with red shiso leaves for color. They are extremely tart, and are considered good for digestion.

Wasabi: Japanese horseradish comes from the root of the wasabi plant that grows in cold mountain streams. It's commonly sold as a pale green powder that is mixed with water or sake to form a thick paste. It is served in a tiny mound with sushi and with sashimi.

Yuzu: A Japanese citrus fruit that looks like a small orange. The aromatic rind is prized for its fragrance in soups. It is in season from late November to January. Substitute fresh lemon or lime.

Suppliers

Asakichi Antiques and Arts

Japan Center, 1730 Geary Boulevard

San Francisco, CA 94115

(415) 921-2147

Asakichi sells many utensils and flower vases especially for Chanoyu. It also carries an assortment of trays and Japanese ceramics that are perfect for the Kaiseki meal. Call for mail order.

Dean & Deluca

560 Broadway

New York, NY 10012

(800) 221-7714

Dean & Deluca should be on everyone's list to visit when in New York. It's a fabulous place, filled with exquisite foods, teas, coffees, spices, herbs, cookbooks, and kitchen utensils, including Japanese tea whisks and teapots. Call for their mail-order catalog.

Katagiri

224 East Fifty-ninth Street

New York, NY 10022

(212) 755-3566

The few essentials for making Kaiseki cuisine can be ordered by phone from this wonderful Japanese market. Its stock includes high-quality kombu, miso, rice vinegar, and dried shiitake mushrooms. It also sells Matcha, fresh powdered green tea for Chanoyu, and bamboo tea whisks.

Sanko Cooking Supply

1785 Buchanan Mall

San Francisco, CA 94115

(415) 922-8331

Call to order Japanese cooking supplies, such as rice molds, vegetable cutters, square pans with removable inserts, and ginger graters. Sanko sells covered lacquer bowls—good-quality plastic ones that are inexpensive and easy to care for.

Takashimaya

693 Fifth Avenue

New York, NY 10022

(212) 350-0100, (800) 453-5908

Takashimaya has a tiny bistro on the ground floor that serves light, appetizing tea-style dishes. At The Tea Box you can buy all sorts of beautifully wrapped and unusual teas, teapots, bamboo tea whisks, and delicate tea ware.

Toraya

17 East Seventy-first Street

New York, NY 10021

(212) 861-1700

(Other shops in Tokyo, Kyoto, and Paris)

This elegant shop and tearoom sells traditional Japanese tea sweets and Matcha. Call for a mail-order catalog, or visit and have a bowl of tea.

Whole Foods Markets

Forty locations throughout the United States

(512) 477-4455

The best-quality fresh fruits, vegetables, fish, and poultry come from this wonderful organic market and natural foods store. You can buy soy sauce and other Japanese ingredients here as well. Call for a list of stores in your area.

Williams-Sonoma

(800) 541-2233

Williams-Sonoma's extensive stock of fine cooking equipment includes bamboo steamers and rice cookers. Call for a catalog and the address of a shop near you.

Yamada Seika Confectionery

1955 Sutter Street

San Francisco, CA 94115

(415) 922-3848

Mr. and Mrs. Yamada make fresh seasonal tea sweets hard to find anywhere else in the United States. The store, near Japantown, is open every day except Mondays. Visit it when you're in San Francisco.

Yaohan Supermarkets

333 South Alameda Street, Los Angeles, CA 90013

595 River Road, Edgewater, NJ 07020

100 East Algonquin Road, Arlington Heights, IL 60005

4240 Kearny Mesa Road, Number 119, San Diego, CA 92111

Inside these vast stores are little stores that sell Japanese cookware, books, ceramics, vegetables, a huge array of pickles, and other foods. They are wonderful places to shop and explore.

The Urasenke Tradition of Tea

Urasenke Konnichian of Kyoto, Japan, has nurtured the rich cultural tradition of Chanoyu since the early seventeenth century. Konnichian created the Urasenke Foundation, Kyoto, in 1964 with the hope of fostering international goodwill through cultural exchange. The foundation's president, Dr. Sōshitsu Sen XV, has traveled extensively since his first visit to the United States in 1951, to introduce the culture of Chanoyu. He lectures at many universities, and three of his books, *Tea Life, Tea Mind*; *Chado: The Japanese Way of Tea*; and *Chanoyu: The Urasenke Tradition of Tea*, have been published in English. With the belief that a world of peace can start with just two individuals, Dr. Sen has established branches in twenty-one cities worldwide.

Contact the Urasenke branch in your area for information about local Urasenke teachers. A national newsletter, *Matsukaze*, is available through the Urasenke Foundation of California.

Urasenke Foundation

Ogawa Teranouchi agaru
Kamikyo-ku
Kyoto, Japan 602
Telephone (075) 431-3111
Telex 5423-263 SENKE J

Urasenke Chanoyu Center

153 East Sixty-ninth Street
New York, NY 10021
(212) 988-6161

Urasenke Foundation of California

2444 Larkin Street
San Francisco, CA 94109
(415) 474-3259

Urasenke Hawaii Branch
245 Saratoga Road
Honolulu, Hawaii 96815

Urasenke Seattle Branch
1910 Thirty-seventh Place East
Seattle, WA 98112
(206) 324-1483

Urasenke Vancouver Branch
3953 West Thirteenth Avenue
Vancouver, British Columbia
Canada V6R 2T1
(604) 244-1560

Bibliography

The History of Tea

Chow, Kit, and Ione Kramer. *All the Tea in China*. San Francisco: China Books, 1990.

Hale, J. R. *Renaissance Exploration*. New York: Norton, 1968.

Hobhouse, Henry. *Seeds of Change*. New York: Harper & Row, 1987.

McCoy, Elin, and John Walker. *Coffee and Tea*. New York: Signet, 1976.

Japanese Art, Literature, and Chanoyu

Ashton, Dore. *Noguchi East and West*. New York: Knopf, 1992.

Cardozo, Sidney, and Misaaki Hirano. *The Art of Rosanjin*. Tokyo, Japan: Kodansha International, 1987.

Carter, Steven D. *Traditional Japanese Poetry: An Anthology*. Stanford, Calif.: Stanford University Press, 1991.

Elison, George, and Bardwell Smith. *Warlords, Artists, & Commoners*. Honolulu, Hawaii: University of Hawaii Press, 1981.

Guth, Christine M. E. *Art, Tea, and Industry*. Princeton, N.J.: Princeton University Press, 1993.

Hall, John Whitney, and Takeshi Toyoda. *Japan in the Muromachi Age*. Berkeley, Calif.: University of California Press, 1977.

Hayashiya, Tatsusaburo, Masao Nakamura, and Seizo Hayashiya. *Japanese Arts and the Tea Ceremony*. Tokyo, Japan: Weatherhill, 1974.

Hayashiya, Seizo. *Chanoyu: The Japanese Tea Ceremony*. New York: Japan Society, 1979.

Hirota, Dennis. *Wind in the Pines: Classic Writings of the Way of Tea as a Buddhist Path*. Fremont, Calif.: Asian Humanities Press, 1995.

Rodd, Laurel Rasplica, with Mary Catherine Henkenius. *Kokinshu: A Collection of Poems Ancient and Modern*. Princeton, N.J.: Princeton University Press, 1984.

Sansom, G. B. *Japan: A Short Cultural History*. Stanford, Calif.: Stanford University Press, 1978.

Sekida, Katsuki. *Two Zen Classics*. Tokyo, Japan: Weatherhill, 1977.

Shimano, Eido Tai. *Points of Departure: Zen Buddhism with a Rinzai View*. Livingston Manor, N.Y.: The Zen Studies Society Press, 1991.

————. *Zen Word, Zen Calligraphy*. Boston, Mass.: Shambhala, 1992.

Sōshitsu Sen XV. *Chado: The Japanese Way of Tea*. Tokyo, Japan: Weatherhill, 1979.

————. *Chanoyu: The Urasenke Tradition of Tea*. Tokyo, Japan: Weatherhill, 1988.

————. *Tea Life, Tea Mind*. Tokyo, Japan: Weatherhill, 1983.

Tsutsui, Hiroichi, and Taka Akanuma. *The Art of Chanoyu: The Urasenke Tradition of Tea*. Kyoto, Japan: The Urasenke Foundation, 1986.

Varley, Paul, and Isao Kumakuro. *Tea in Japan: Essays on the History of Chanoyu*. Honolulu, Hawaii: University of Hawaii Press, 1989.

Cooking

Beck, Simone, Louisette Bertholle, and Julia Child. *Mastering the Art of French Cooking*. New York: Knopf, 1966.

Tsuchiya, Yoshio. *A Feast for the Eyes: The Japanese Art of Food Arrangement*. Tokyo, Japan: Kodansha International, 1985.

Tsuji, Kaichi. *Kaiseki: Zen Tastes in Japanese Cooking*. Kyoto, Japan: Tankosha, 1972.

Tsuji, Shizuo. *Japanese Cooking: A Simple Art*. Tokyo, Japan: Kodansha International, 1980.

Waters, Alice. *The Chez Panisse Menu Cookbook*. New York: Random House, 1982.

Yoneda, Soei. *The Heart of Zen Cuisine*. Tokyo, Japan: Kodansha International, 1982.

Periodicals

Matsukaze: Chanoyu Journal for the Urasenke Foundation of North America. Matsukaze literally means "pine wind." The phrase "listen to the wind in the pines" has long been used as a koan questioning the nature of perception. In tea, this phrase describes a certain sound of boiling water. Wind is an agent that carries sound, scent, and messages to distant friends. As a journal, *Matsukaze* carries news of Chanoyu in North

America. For more information contact the Urasenke Foundation, 2444 Larkin Street, San Francisco, CA 94109.

Chanoyu Quarterly. Urasenke Foundation. More than 80 issues written in English, covering the art and aesthetics of Chanoyu. To order, write: Urasenke Chanoyu Center, 153 East Sixty-ninth Street, New York, NY 10021.

Momo No Sono. A beautiful handmade quarterly publication devoted to tea and poetics. Write to 117 Peralta Avenue, San Francisco, CA 94110.

Scientific Studies of Tea

Chow, Kit, and Ione Kramer. *All the Tea in China.* San Francisco: China Books, 1990. Detailed chapter on tea and your health.

Gao, Y. T., and W. J. Blot. "Reduced Risk of Esophageal Cancer Associated with Green Tea Consumption." *Journal of the National Cancer Institute* 86(II) 1994.

Han, J. "Highlights of the Cancer Chemoprevention Studies in China." *Preventative Medicine* 22(5) 1993.

Komori, A. "Anticarcinogenic Activity of Green Tea Polyphenols." *Japanese Journal of Clinical Oncology* 23(3) 1993.

Schwarz, B. "Coffee, Tea, and Lifestyle." *Preventative Medicine* 23(3) 1994.

"Scientists Optimistic About Tea." *Environmental Nutrition* (May 1996). The results of various scientific studies that strengthen the connection between drinking tea and good health.

Steinman, David. "Why You Should Drink Green Tea." *Natural Health Magazine* (March/April 1994). Fight cavities, bad breath, flu—even heart disease and cancer—with this simple beverage.

"Tea Ceremony Is Therapeutic." *The Wall Street Journal,* 18 December 1990. Akira Fukao of Tohoku University surveyed 3,380 women who practiced tea ceremony to investigate possibilities that green tea contains cancer-preventing ingredients.

University of California at Berkeley Wellness Letter 10, no. 12 (September 1994). A report on the polyphenols in green tea that may prevent cancer.

Weininger, Jean. "Tea: Soothing Body and Soul." *San Francisco Chronicle,* 10 May 1995. A report on the health value of tea.

Index

Author's Note

If you've enjoyed reading this book and you'd like more information about tea and Chanoyu, visit *The World in a Bowl of Tea*'s website at:

http://www.e-media.com/tea

Or write to:

Bettina Vitell
2130 Fillmore Street, #288
San Francisco, CA 94115